*Routledge Revivals*

# Trade, Transport and Society in the Ancient World

This book, first published in 1992, presents an introduction to the nature of trade and transport in antiquity through a selection of translated literary, papyrological, epigraphical and legal sources. These texts illustrate a range of aspects of ancient trade and transport: from the role of the authorities, to the status of traders, to the capacity and speed of ancient ships.

It is clear that the actual means of transportation were crucial; the book illustrates the limitations of ancient transport technology and the consequences for the development of commerce. It focuses first on different aspects of transport over land and then on transport by river and concludes with a discussion of several aspects of ancient seafaring.

*Trade, Transport and Society in the Ancient World: A Sourcebook* is ideal for students of ancient history.

# Trade, Transport and Society in the Ancient World

## A Sourcebook

Fik Meijer and Onno van Nijf

Routledge
Taylor & Francis Group

First published in 1992
by Routledge

This edition first published in 2015 by Routledge
2 Park Square, Milton Park, Abingdon, Oxon, OX14 4RN
and by Routledge
711 Third Avenue, New York, NY 10017

*Routledge is an imprint of the Taylor & Francis Group, an informa business*



A Library of Congress record exists under LC control number: 91046010

ISBN 13: 978-1-138-82659-5 (hbk)
ISBN 13: 978-1-315-73919-9 (ebk)
ISBN 13: 978-1-138-82660-1 (pbk)

# Trade, Transport and Society in the Ancient World

## A sourcebook

Fik Meijer
and
Onno van Nijf

ROUTLEDGE
London and New York

First published 1992
by Routledge
11 New Fetter Lane, London EC4P 4EE

Simultaneously published in the USA and Canada
by Routledge
a division of Routledge, Chapman and Hall Inc.
29 West 35th Street, New York, NY 10001



Typeset in 10 on 12 point Times by
Falcon Typographic Art Ltd, Fife, Scotland
Printed in Great Britain by
Clays Ltd, St Ives plc



*British Library Cataloguing in Publication Data*
Meijer, Fik
Trade, transport and society in the ancient world.
I. Title II. Nijf, Onno van
380.5

*Library of Congress Cataloging in Publication Data*
Meijer, Fik.
Trade, transport and society in the ancient world: a sourcebook/Fik Meijer and Onno van Nijf.
p. cm.
Includes bibliographical references and index.
1. Greece – Commerce – History – Sources. 2. Transportation – Greece – History – Sources. 3. Rome – Commerce – History – Sources. 4. Transportation – Rome – History – Sources. I. Nijf, Onno van. II. Title.
HF373. M45 1992
380'. 093 – dc20 71 71 71 71 71 91–46010

ISBN 0–415–00344–X
0–415–00345–8 (pbk)

# Contents

# Preface

Interest in the economic history of antiquity has been increasing during the last decades. The publication in 1973 of M.I. Finley's *The Ancient Economy*, in particular, has been a strong stimulus for further research. Much work has been done on Finley's concept of a primitive economy, which has consequently been refined in many respects. Scholars agree that the ancient world was primarily agrarian in nature. Most of those who produced agricultural products did so for their own use, a situation which continued throughout antiquity. The cities, however, became increasingly important: markets arose and the scale of agricultural production increased. As a result, trade and industry acquired a more significant role, as has been clearly demonstrated, for example, in P. Garnsey, K. Hopkins and C.R. Whittaker, *Trade in the Ancient Economy* (London 1983). One consequence of this recent perception of the importance of trade has been that this aspect of the ancient economy has been incorporated in university curricula.

This book, intended for undergraduate students and for the general reader with a serious interest in ancient history, differs from other treatments of the ancient economy in that the emphasis is on trade and the ways in which it was carried out. The starting-point is formed by the ancient sources concerning trade and transport. These are not presented as a loose collection of passages from literary works, inscriptions and papyri, but are organized thematically.

Part I, on the ideology and practice of ancient trade, deals first with Greek and Roman value systems, and élite attitudes towards trade. The remaining chapters of Part I present the realities of trade in Homeric and archaic Greece, Athens and the Athenian Empire, the Greek world outside Athens, Ptolemaic Egypt, and finally the Roman Empire. Special attention will be given to other forms of exchange than commercial exchange, the attitudes of the authorities towards trade, the status of traders and the ways in which trade was organized.

Part II deals with the most important commodities of ancient trade: grain, wool and textiles, wine and oil, building materials and slaves. This part concludes with a discussion of the trade between the Graeco-Roman world and India and the Orient, and the trade with the northern barbarians.

Part III deals with transport and the means of transportation. It illustrates the limitations of ancient transport technology and the consequences for the development of commerce. It focuses first on different aspects of transport over land and then on transport by river. It concludes with a discussion of several aspects of ancient seafaring.

A book with so broad a subject cannot but suffer from incompleteness. We had to limit not only the number of topics, but also the number of texts illustrating each topic. We can only hope that our selection will not appear too arbitrary.

Since neither author is a native speaker of English it has been decided to make frequent use of existing English translations. We would like to record our gratitude to the copyright holders for their permission to use their translations. Translations borrowed by us are mentioned at the end of the texts. In some cases slight alterations were made; this is indicated below the text. Complete references to the translations can be found in the acknowledgements. Where no translator is mentioned translations are our own. As a rule, Greek personal and geographical names have been rendered in their Latinized form. It was not possible, however, to be fully consistent. Titles of ancient sources are normally given in English, apart from cases where this could lead to confusion. There the Latin title is given. In the use of square and round brackets, generally we follow the translators. We use square brackets to indicate additions by the editor of words or parts of words which were once inscribed on the stone, but are no longer legible (the standard epigraphic/papyrological practice); round brackets are used (a) to indicate additions by the editor of words or parts of words which were never inscribed in the text, but which are essential for the understanding and (b) for our own, or the editor's explanations of words.

P. Glare, J.M. Reynolds, P.J. Sijpesteijn, S. Voutsaki, C.R. Whittaker and K.A. Worp have read and commented upon the whole text or parts of it. They have given valuable advice and have saved us from many errors. Rosamund Annetts has painstakingly improved our English. The lion's share of the typing was done by Hetty de Schepper. We would like to thank them all for their help. All remaining errors are, of course, completely our responsibility.

Finally we would like to thank Harry Pleket, not only for his help with this book, but for everything he taught us over the years and for his warm support and friendship. To him we dedicate this book.

Amsterdam, November 1991

# Acknowledgements

Acknowledgements are due to the following publishers for permission to reproduce translations.

**LOEB CLASSICAL LIBRARY**
(Harvard University Press; William Heinemann)

J.C. Rolfe's translation of *Ammianus Marcellinus* (1986) in no. 188
K.J. Maidment's translation of *Minor Attic Orators* (Andocides) (1982) in no. 51
H. White's translation of *Appian's Roman History* (1979) in no. 231
C.B. Gulick's translation of *Athenaeus. The Deipnosophists* (1987) in nos 12, 83 and 86
L.H.G. Greenwood's translation of *Cicero: The Verrine Orations* (1935) in no. 14
N.H. Watts' translation of *Cicero. The Speeches* (1945) in no. 128
J.H. Vince's translation of *Demosthenes* (1978) in nos 54, 61, 62, 66, 68, 69, 70, 118 and 119
E. Cary's translation of *Dio Cassius. Roman History* (1980) in no. 235
J.W. Cohoon's translation of *Dio Chrysostomus* (1971) in nos 78, 99 and 115
C.H. Oldfather's translation of *Diodorus Siculus* (1962) in nos 144 and 161
E. Evelyn White's translation of *The Homeric Hymns* (1936) in no. 30
G. Norlin's translation of *Isocrates* (1980) in no. 50
W.R.M. Lamb's translation of *Lysias* (1988) in nos 63 and 120
P. Nixon's translation of *Plautus* (1957) in no. 96
H. Rackman's translation of *Pliny. Natural History* (1983) in nos 126, 131, 167, 168 and 199

W. Melmoth's translation of *Pliny. Letters* (1948) in nos 191 and 236 (vol. I (1957), vol. II (1958))
B. Perrin's translation of *Plutarch. The Parallel Lives* (1985) in nos 42 and 145
W.R. Paton's translation of *Polybius. Histories* (1978) in nos 71 and 74
H.L. Jones' translation of *Strabo* (1983, 1988) in nos 39, 73, 76, 134, 135, 152, 153, 157, 160, 162, 163, 180, 187, 219, 221 and 232
F. Granger's translation of *Vitruvius. De Architectura* (1956) in no. 234
E.C. Marchant's translation of *Xenophon. Scripta Minora* (1962) in no. 57
C.L. Brownson's translation of *Xenophon. Hellenica* (1985) in no. 151

**PENGUIN BOOKS**

R. Graves' translation of *Apuleius. The Golden Ass* (1990) in no. 215
A.H. Sommerstein's translation of *Aristophanes. Wealth* (1986) in no. 156
A. De Sélincourt's translation of *Herodotus. The Histories* (1972) in nos 11, 36, 37, 38, 40, 43, 117, 142, 154, 177, 208 and 226
M. Hammond's translation of *Homer. Iliad* (1987) in nos 27, 29 and 141
E.V. Rieu's translation of *Homer. Odyssey* (1946) in nos 2, 3, 25, 26, 27, 28, 29, 31, 32, 141 and 225
A. Birley's translation of *The Lives of the Later Caesars* (1976) in no. 98
A. De Sélincourt's translation of *Livy. The War with Hannibal* (1965) in no. 13
P. Levi's translation of *Pausanias. Guide to Greece* (1979) in no. 228
J.P. Sullivan's translation of *Petronius. Satyricon* (1974) in no. 104
J. Scott-Kilvert's translation of *Plutarch. Makers of Rome* (1987) in nos 95 and 181
R. Graves' translation of *Suetonius. The Twelve Caesars* (1979) in nos 129 and 222
M. Grant's translation of *Tacitus. The Annals of Imperial Rome* (1989) in no. 192

**B.T. BATSFORD, LONDON**

M.M. Austin's and P. Vidal-Naquet's translation in *Economic and Social History of Ancient Greece* (1973) in no. 47

**E.J. BRILL, LEIDEN**

C.A. Behr's translation of *Aelius Aristides. The Complete Works* (1981) in no. 112

**CAMBRIDGE UNIVERSITY PRESS**

M.M. Austin's translations in *The Hellenistic World from Alexander to the Roman Conquest* (1981) in nos 72, 77, 80, 81, 85 and 121
Ph. Harding's translation in *From the End of the Peloponnesian War to the Battle of Ipsus* (1985) in no. 60

**CAMBRIDGE UNIVERSITY PRESS/ OXFORD UNIVERSITY PRESS**

Translations of *The Revised English Bible* in nos 23 and 217

**R. HABELT, BONN**

J. Rea's translation in *ZPE* (1982) in no. 108
L. Casson's translation in *ZPE* (1990) in no. 166

**JOHNS HOPKINS UNIVERSITY PRESS, BALTIMORE**

Ch.W. Fornara's translation in *Archaic Times to the End of the Peloponnesian War* (1977) in nos 48, 122 and 143
T. Frank's translation in *An Economic Survey of Ancient Rome* (1934–40) in no. 186
C.P. Jones' translation in *AJP* (1989) in no. 113

**OXFORD UNIVERSITY PRESS**

A. Fitzgerald's translation of *The Letters of Synesius* (1926) in no. 218
M. West's translation of *Hesiod. Works and Days* (1988) in no. 4
E.S. Forster's and B. Jowett's translations of *Aristotle* in *The Works of Aristotle translated into English under the editorship of W.D. Ross* (1921) in nos 8 and 9

F. Homes Dudden's translation of *Ambrose* in *The Life and Times of St. Ambrose* (1934) in no. 24
E.G. Hardy's translation of *Roman Laws and Charters* (1924) in no. 189

**PRINCETON UNIVERSITY PRESS**

C. Pharr's translation of *The Theodosian Code* (1952) in nos 174 and 175
L. Casson's translation of *Periplus Maris Erythraei* (1989) in no. 165
L. Casson's translation of *Achilles Tatius* and *Athenaeus* (1972) in *Ships and Seamanship in the Ancient World* in nos 197 and 224

**RANDOM CENTURY GROUP LTD, LONDON**

J.M. Moore's translation in *Aristotle and Xenophon on Democracy and Oligarchy* (1975) in nos 10, 46 and 56

**SCHOLARS PRESS, ITHACA, NEW YORK**

L. Casson's translation in the *Bulletin of the American Society of Papyrologists* (1990) in no. 202

**SOCIETY FOR THE PROMOTION OF ROMAN STUDIES**

S. Mitchell's translation in *JRS* (1976) in no. 176

**THE AMERICAN PHILOLOGICAL ASSOCIATION**

J.H. Oliver's translation in *The Ruling Power* (*Transactions of the American Philological Association*, 1953) in no. 148

We have tried in vain to trace the copyright holders of:
M.N. Tod's translation in *JHS* (1934) in no. 79
A.E. Taylor's translation of *Plato. The Laws* (London, 1934) in nos 5 and 6
R. Crawley's translation of *Thucydides. The Peloponnesian War* (New York, 1951) in nos 1, 33, 49, and 195

# Measures, weights and coins

## MEASURES OF LENGTH

| | |
|---|---|
| finger (Gk *daktylos*, Lat. *digitus*) | = 1.9 cm |
| feet (Gk *pous*, Lat. *pes*) | = 30 cm |
| cubit (Gk *pechus*, Lat. *cubitus*) | = 45 cm |
| pace (Lat. *passus*) | = 1.48 m |
| fathom (Gk *orguia*) | = 1.80 m |
| plethrum (Gk *plethron*, Lat. *plethrum*) | = 30 m |
| stade (furlong) (Gk *stadion*) | = 180 m |
| Roman mile (Lat. *mille passus*) | = 1,480 m |
| parasang (Gk *parasanges*) | = *c*. 5.5 km |
| schoenum (Gk *schoinos*, Lat. *schoenum*) | = *c*. 10.5 km |

## MEASURES OF VOLUME

### Dry measures

| | |
|---|---|
| artaba (Gk *artaba*) | = 39 l |
| in late antiquity | = 29 l |
| medimnos (Gk *medimnos*) | = 52.53 l |
| Hekteus (Gk *hekteus*) | = 8.72 l |
| modius (Lat. *modius*) | = 8.74 l |

A modius castrensis = 1.5 modius Italicus

### Liquid measures

| | |
|---|---|
| metrete (Gk *metretes*) | = 39.39 l |
| amphora | = 26.2 l |

Converting the measures of volume to kilograms the following guide numbers can be used:

| | | |
|---|---|---|
| artaba grain | | = *c.* 30.2 kg |
| | in late antiquity | = *c.* 21.5 kg |
| metrete oil | | = *c.* 35.1 kg |
| medimnos grain | | = *c.* 40 kg |
| modius grain | | = *c.* 6.7 kg |
| hekteus grain | | = *c.* 6.7 kg |

## WEIGHTS

| | |
|---|---|
| Roman pound (Lat.: *libra*) | = 327.45 g |
| talent (Gk: *talanton*) | = 26.2 kg |

## COINS

**Greek:** 6 obols = 1 drachma
100 drachmas = 1 mina
60 minas = 1 talent

A stater = 4 drachmas (Athens) or 2 drachmas (elsewhere)

**Roman:** 4 asses = 1 sestertius (bronze)
4 sestertii = 1 denarius (silver)
25 denarii = 1 aureus (gold)

# Abbreviations

| | |
|---|---|
| *AE* | *L'Année Epigraphique* |
| *AJP* | *American Journal of Philology* |
| *BGU* | *Berliner Griechischer Urkunden (Aegyptische Urkunden aus den Königlichen Museen zu Berlin)* |
| *CIL* | *Corpus Inscriptionum Latinarum* |
| *C. Ord. Ptol.* | M.T. Lenger, *Corpus des Ordonnances des Ptolemées* |
| *ESAR* | T. Frank (ed.), *An Economic Survey of Ancient Rome*, 5 vols (1933–40) |
| *IG* | *Inscriptiones Graecae* |
| *IGSK* | *Inschriften griechischer Städte aus Kleinasien* |
| *ILS* | *Inscriptiones Latinae Selectae*, ed. H. Dessau |
| *JHS* | *Journal of Hellenic Studies* |
| *JRS* | *Journal of Roman Studies* |
| LCL | Loeb Classical Library |
| Meiggs and Lewis | R. Meiggs and D.M. Lewis, *A Selection of Greek Historical Inscriptions to the End of the Fifth Century* BC (1958) |
| *PCPS* | *Proceedings of the Cambridge Philosophical Society* |
| *P. Cairo Zen.* | *Zenon Papyri* |
| *P. Erasm.* | *Papyri Erasmianae* |
| *P. Flor.* | *Papyri greco-egizii, Papiri Fiorentini* |
| *P. Hibeh* | *The Hibeh Papyri* |
| *P. Lond.* | *Greek Papyri in the British Museum* |
| *P. Mich.* | *Michigan Papyri*. Vol. I is often referred to as *P. Mich. Zen.* (*Zenon Papyri*) |
| *P. Tebt.* | *The Tebtunis Papyri* |

| | |
|---|---|
| *P. Vind.* | *Wiener Papyri* |
| *REG* | *Revue des Études Grecques* |
| *SEG* | *Supplementum Epigraphicum Graecum* |
| *SIG*[3] | W. Dittenberger (ed.), *Sylloge Inscriptionum Graecarum*, 3rd edn |
| *TAM* | *Tituli Asiae Minoris* |
| Tod II | M.N. Tod, *A Selection of Greek Historical Inscriptions, II. From 403 to 323 BC* (1948) |
| *TAPA* | *Transactions and Proceedings of the American Philological Association* |
| *ZPE* | *Zeitschrift für Papyrologie und Epigraphik* |

# Part I

# Ideology and practice of ancient trade

# 1 Greek and Roman values

The ideology of the landowning aristocracies of antiquity finds expression in Greek and Latin literature. Often praise is heaped upon agriculture, but trade is only mentioned as an afterthought, or not at all. Occasionally the negative aspects of trade are dealt with in more detail. Some authors merely sum up the traditional objections to trade; others deal with it in a more philosophical way.

## I GREEK VALUES

### 1 Thucydides I.2.1–2

The Athenian historian Thucydides (fifth century BC) looks back to the early days of Greek history, and describes a situation that differs widely from circumstances prevailing in his own days:

For instance, it is evident that the country now called Hellas had in ancient times no settled population; on the contrary, migrations were of frequent occurrence, the several tribes readily abandoning their homes under the pressure of superior numbers. Without commerce, without freedom of communication either by land or sea, cultivating no more of their territory than the exigencies of life required, destitute of capital, never planting their land (for they could not tell when an invader might not come and take it all away, and when he did come they had no walls to stop him), thinking that the necessities of daily sustenance could be supplied at one place as well as another, they cared little for shifting their habitation, and consequently neither built large cities nor attained to any other form of greatness.

(trans. Crawley)

## 2 Homer, *Odyssey* XIV.288–9

In the world described by Homer regular trade existed on a small scale. The typical specialist trader was an outsider, like the Phoenician of this fragment. He was treated with distrust, even though his merchandise was welcome. Here Odysseus has returned to Ithaca after a long absence. He tells his trusted swineherd Eumaeus of his travels, and describes a Phoenician, whom he has met in Egypt.

But in the course of the eighth, I fell in with a rascally Phoenician, a thieving rogue who had already done a deal of mischief in the world.

(trans. Rieu)

## 3 Homer, *Odyssey* XV.415–17

Eumaeus, who was sold as a slave to the father of Odysseus by Phoenician merchants, shares his feelings.

One day the island was visited by a party of Phoenicians – famous sailors, but greedy rogues – with a whole cargo of trinkets in their black ship.

(trans. Rieu)

## 4 Hesiod, *Works and Days* 618–94

Around 700 BC Hesiod wrote his *Works and Days*. The poem is partially directed against his brother Perses, who has robbed him of part of his patrimony. Hesiod deals thoroughly with the social and economic problems that confront the farmer, and offers practical and moral advice. He praises the *esthlos bios*, the noble way of life of the countryman, and expresses his disapproval of the hazards of maritime trade.

If now the desire to go to sea (disagreeable as it is) has hold of you: when the Pleiades, running before Orion's grim strength, are plunging into the misty sea, then the blasts of every kind of wind rage; at this time do not keep ships on the wine-faced sea, but work the earth assiduously, as I tell you. Pull the ship on to land and pack it with stones all round to withstand the fury of the wet-blowing winds, taking out the plug so that heaven's rains do not cause rot. Lay away all the tackle under lock in your house, tidily stowing the wings of the seagoing vessel; hang the well-crafted steering-oar up in the smoke; and wait till the time for sailing comes.

Then drag the swift ship to the sea, and in it arrange your cargo fittingly so that you may win profit for your return: just as my father and yours, foolish Perses, used to sail in ships in want of fair livelihood. And one day he came here, making the long crossing from Aeolian Cyme in his dark ship, not running from riches, nor from wealth and prosperity, but from evil poverty, which Zeus dispenses to men. And he settled near Helicon in a miserable village, Ascra, bad in winter, foul in summer, good at no time.

But you, Perses, must attend to all tasks in season, and in the matter of seafaring above all. Compliment a small ship, but put your cargo in a big one: bigger will be the cargo, bigger the extra gain, provided that the winds withhold their ill blasts.

When you want to escape debt and joyless hunger by turning your blight-witted heart to trade, I will show you the measure of the resounding sea – quite without instruction as I am either in seafaring or in ships; for as to ships, I have never yet sailed the broad sea, except to Euboea from Aulis, the way the Achaeans once came when they waited through the winter and gathered a great army from holy Greece against Troy of the fair women. There to the funeral games for warlike Amphidamas and to Chalcis I crossed, and many were the prizes announced and displayed by the sons of that valiant; where I may say that I was victorious in poetry and won a tripod with ring handles. That I dedicated to the Muses of Helicon, in the original place where they set me on the path of fine singing. That is all my experience of dowelled ships, but even so I will tell the design of Zeus the aegis-bearer, since the Muses have taught me to make song without limit.

For fifty days after the solstice, when the summer has entered its last stage, the season of fatigue, then is the time for mortals to sail. You are not likely to smash your ship, nor the sea to destroy the crew, unless it be that of set mind Poseidon the earth-shaker or Zeus king of the immortals wants to destroy them, for in their hands lies the outcome of good and bad things alike. At that time the breezes are well defined and the sea harmless. Then without anxiety, trusting the winds, drag your swift ship into the sea and put all the cargo aboard. But make haste to come home again as quickly as you can, and do not wait for the new wine and the autumn rains, the onset of winter and the fearsome blasts of the South Wind, which stirs up the sea as it comes with heaven's plentiful rains of autumn, and makes the waves rough.

There is another time for men to sail in the spring. As soon as the size of the crow's footprint is matched by the aspect of the leaves on the end of the fig-branch, then the sea is suitable for embarkation. This is the spring sailing. I do not recommend it;

it is not to my heart's liking. A snatched sailing: you would have difficulty in avoiding trouble. But men do even that in their folly, because property is as life to wretched mortals. But it is a fearful thing to die among the waves. I suggest you bear all this in mind, as I tell you it.

And do not put all your substance in ships' holds, but leave the greater part and ship the lesser; for it is a fearful thing to meet with disaster among the waves of the sea, and a fearful thing if you put too great a burden upon your cart and smash the axle and the cargo is spoiled. Observe due measure; opportuneness is best in everything.

(trans. West)

### 5 Plato, *Laws* IV.704b5–705b8

In the *Laws*, his last work, Plato (427–347 BC) offers a blueprint for his ideal state. In his opinion one consideration should be its location. Proximity to the sea offers more disadvantages than advantages.

Had it to be on the coast, well furnished with harbours and ill off for many of its necessaries, not productive of all, we should need a mighty protector and lawgivers who were more than men to prevent the development of much refined vice in consequence of such a situation. As it is, there is comfort in those eighty stadia. Even so, the site is nearer to the sea than it should be, all the more as you say it is well provided with a harbour. Still, we ought to be thankful for even so much. It is agreeable enough to have the sea at one's door in daily life; but, for all that, it is, in very truth, a 'briny' and bitter 'neighbour'. It fills a city with wholesale traffic and retail huckstering, breeds shifty and distrustful habits of soul, and so makes a society distrustful and unfriendly within itself as well as towards mankind at large. In view of this situation, there is further comfort, however, in the universal productiveness of our site.

(trans. Taylor)

### 6 Plato, *Laws* XII.952d–953e

Traders from other cities would better be kept outside the city walls.

We are next to consider the welcome to be given to a visitor from abroad. The foreign visitors of whom account must be taken are of four sorts. First, and everlastingly, a guest who will pay his incessant calls, for the most part, in the summer, like a bird of passage; most of his kind are, in fact, just like winged creatures in the way they come flying overseas, at the proper season, on their profitable business errands. He shall be admitted by officials appointed for his benefit, to our market-place, harbours, and certain public buildings erected near the city but outside its walls. The officials will take care to prevent the introduction of novelties by these guests, and will administer proper justice to them, but shall keep their intercourse with them within the strict bounds of necessity.

(trans. Taylor)

## 7 Xenophon, *Oeconomicus* V.17

The word 'economics' is derived from a Greek word: *oikonomia*. Yet when in the fourth century Xenophon published his *Oeconomicus* and Aristotle his *Economics*, the subject was by no means an analysis of the 'economic system as an enormous conglomeration of interdependent markets'.[1] The subject-matter was the management of the *oikos*, the household, or management, administration and organization of larger units.

The *Oeconomicus* of Xenophon is a Socratic dialogue on the running of an agricultural estate. Agriculture is described as the only activity befitting a gentleman. It is praised for having a positive effect on a man's character, deriving from the fact that agriculture is the only truly self-sufficient activity.

Whoever said that husbandry is the mother and nurse of all the other arts spoke finely indeed. For when husbandry goes well, all the other arts also flourish, but when the earth is compelled to lie barren, the other arts almost cease to exist, at sea as well as on the earth.

*NOTE*

1 M.I. Finley, *The Ancient Economy*, London 1985², 22.

## 8 Aristotle, *Economics* II.1.1–6

The central problem of Aristotle's *Oeconomica* is the way in which individual landowners, administrators and rulers managed their budgets. His main principle is the common-sense observation that expenditure should never exceed revenue. He distinguishes between four types of 'economy':

He who intends to practise economy aright ought to be fully acquainted with the places in which his labour lies and to be naturally endowed with good parts and deliberately industrious and upright; for if he is lacking in any of these respects, he will make many mistakes in the business which he takes in hand.

Now there are four kinds of economy, that of the king (Royal

Economy), that of the provincial governor (Satrapic Economy), that of the city (Political Economy), and that of the individual (Personal Economy). This is a broad method of division; and we shall find that the other forms of economy fall within it.

Of these the Royal is the most important and the simplest, the Political is the most varied and the easiest, the Personal the least important and the most varied. They must necessarily have most of their characteristics in common; but it is the points which are peculiar to each kind that we must consider. Let us therefore examine Royal Economy first. It is universal in its scope, but has four special departments – the coinage, exports, imports, and expenditure. To take each of these separately: in regard to the coinage, I mean the question as to what coin should be struck and when it should be of a high and when of a low value; in the matter of exports and imports, what commodities it will be advantageous to receive from the satraps under the Royal rule and dispose of and when; in regard to expenditure, what expenses ought to be curtailed and when, and whether one should pay what is expended in coin or in commodities which have an equivalent value.

Let us next take Satrapic Economy. Here we find six kinds of revenue: from land, from the peculiar products of the district, from merchandise, from taxes, from cattle, and from all other sources. Of these the first and most important is that which comes from land (which some call tax on land-produce, others tithe); next in importance is the revenue from peculiar products, from gold, or silver, or copper, or anything else which is found in a particular locality; thirdly comes that derived from merchandise; fourthly, the revenue from the cultivation of the soil and from market-dues; fifthly, that which comes from cattle, which is called tax on animal produce or tithe; and sixthly, that which is derived from other sources, which is called the poll-tax or tax on handicraft.

Thirdly, let us examine the economy of the city. Here the most important source of revenue is from the peculiar products of the country, next comes that derived from merchandise and customs, and lastly that which comes from the ordinary taxes.

Fourthly and lastly, let us take Personal Economy. Here we find wide divergences, because economy is not necessarily always practised with one aim in view. It is the least important kind of economy, because the incomings and expenses are small. Here the main source of revenue is the land, next other kinds of property, and thirdly investments of money.

Further, there is a consideration which is common to all branches of economy and which calls for the most careful attention, especially in personal economy, namely, that the expenditure must not exceed the income.

(trans. Forster)

### 9 Aristotle, *Politics* I.3.1–18

Greek thinking about economic activities was closely connected to ideas about the *polis*. Aristotle's analysis of production and consumption is framed within the limits of his analysis of the city-state. *Chrematistikè*, or the art of money-making, is presented as an unnatural activity, contrary to the ideology of the *polis*. In his *Politics* he elaborates on an attempt to reconcile the reality to his philosophical ideal.

Let us now inquire into property generally, and into the art of getting wealth, in accordance with our usual method, for a slave has been shown to be a part of property. The first question is whether the art of getting wealth is the same with the art of managing a household or a part of it, or instrumental to it; and if the last, whether in the way that the art of making shuttles is instrumental to the art of weaving, or in the way that the casting of bronze is instrumental to the art of the statuary, for they are not instrumental in the same way, but the one provides tools and the other material; and by material I mean the substratum out of which any work is made; thus wool is the material of the weaver, bronze of the statuary. Now it is easy to see that the art of household management is not identical with the art of getting wealth, for the one uses the material which the other provides. For the art which uses household stores can be no other than the art of household management. There is, however, a doubt whether the art of getting wealth is a part of household management or a distinct art. If the getter of wealth has to consider whence wealth and property can be procured, but there are many sorts of property and riches, then are husbandry, and the care and provision of food in general, parts of the wealth-getting art or distinct arts? Again, there are many sorts of food, and therefore there are many kinds of lives both of animals and men; they must all have food, and the differences in their food have made differences in their ways of life. For of beasts, some are gregarious, others are solitary; they live in the way which is best adapted to sustain them, accordingly as they are carnivorous or herbivorous or omnivorous: and their habits are determined for them by nature in such a manner that they may obtain with greater facility the food of their choice. But, as different species have different tastes, the same things are not naturally pleasant to all of them; and therefore the lives of carnivorous or herbivorous animals further differ among themselves. In the lives of men too there is a great difference. The laziest are shepherds, who lead an idle life, and get their subsistence without trouble from tame animals; their flocks having to wander from place to place in search of pasture, they are compelled to follow them, cultivating a sort of living farm. Others support themselves by hunting, which is of different kinds. Some, for example, are brigands, others, who dwell near lakes or marshes or rivers or a sea in which there are fish, are fishermen, and others live by the pursuit of birds or wild beasts. The greater number obtain a living from the cultivated fruits of the soil. Such are the modes of subsistence which prevail among those whose industry springs up of itself, and whose food is not acquired by exchange and retail trade – there is the shepherd, the husbandman, the brigand, the fisherman, the hunter. Some gain a comfortable maintenance out of two employments, eking out the deficiencies of one of them by another: thus the life of a shepherd may be combined with that of a brigand, the life of a farmer with that of a hunter. Other modes of life are similarly combined in any way which the needs of men may require. Property, in the sense of a bare livelihood, seems to be given by nature herself to all, both when they are first born, and when they are grown up. For some animals bring forth, together with their offspring, so much food as will last until they are able to supply themselves; of this the vermiparous or oviparous animals are an instance; and the viviparous animals have up to a certain time a supply of food for their young in themselves, which is called milk. In like manner we may infer that, after the birth of animals, plants exist for their sake, and that the other animals exist for the sake of man, the tame for use and food, the wild, if not all, at least the greater part of them, for food, and for the provision of clothing and various instruments. Now if nature makes nothing incomplete, and nothing in vain, the inference must be that she has made all animals for the sake of man. And so, in one point of view, the art of war is a natural art of acquisition, for the art of acquisition includes hunting, an art which we ought to practise against wild beasts, and against men who, though intended by nature to be governed, will not submit; for war of such a kind is naturally just.

Of the art of acquisition then there is one kind which by nature is a part of the management of a household, in so far as the art of household management must either find ready to hand, or itself provide, such things necessary to life, and useful for the community of the family or state, as can be stored. They are the elements of true riches; for the amount of property which is needed for a good life is not unlimited, although Solon in one of his poems says that

'No bound to riches has been fixed for man.'[1]

But there is a boundary fixed, just as there is in the other arts; for the instruments of any art are never unlimited, either in number or size, and riches may be defined as a number of instruments to be used in a household or in a state. And so we see that there is a natural art of acquisition which is practised by managers of households and by statesmen, and what is the reason of this.

There is another variety of the art of acquisition which is commonly and rightly called an art of wealth-getting, and has in fact suggested the notion that riches and property have no limit. Being nearly connected with the preceding, it is often identified with it. But though they are not very different, neither are they the same. The kind already described is given by nature, the other is gained by experience and art.

Let us begin our discussion of the question with the following considerations:

Of everything which we possess there are two uses: both belong to the thing as such, but not in the same manner, for one is the proper, and the other the improper or secondary use of it. For example, a shoe is used for wear, and is used for exchange; both are uses of the shoe. He who gives a shoe in exchange for money or food to him who wants one, does indeed use the shoe as a shoe, but this is not its proper or primary purpose, for a shoe is not made to be an object of barter. The same may be said of all possessions, for the art of exchange extends to all of them, and it arises at first from what is natural, from the circumstance that some have too little, others too much. Hence we may infer that retail trade is not a natural part of the art of getting wealth; had it been so, men would have ceased to exchange when they had enough. In the first community, indeed, which is the family, this art is obviously of no use, but it begins to be useful when the society increases. For the members of the family originally had all things in common; later, when the family divided into parts, the parts shared in many things, and different parts in different things, which they had to give in exchange for what they wanted, a kind of barter which is still practised among barbarous nations who exchange with one another the necessaries of life and nothing more; giving and receiving wine, for example, in exchange for corn, and the like. This sort of barter is not part of the wealth-getting art and is not contrary to nature, but is needed for the satisfaction of men's natural wants. The other or more complex form of exchange grew, as might have been inferred, out of the simpler. When the inhabitants of one country became more dependent on those of another, and they imported what they needed, and exported what they had too much of, money necessarily came into use. For the various necessaries of life are not easily carried about, and hence men agreed to employ in their dealings with each other something which was intrinsically useful and easily applicable to the purposes of life, for example, iron, silver, and the like. Of this the value was at first measured simply by size and weight, but in process of time they put a stamp upon it, to save the trouble of weighing and to mark the value.

When the use of coin had once been discovered, out of the barter of necessary articles arose the other art of wealth-getting, namely retail trade; which was at first probably a simple matter, but became more complicated as soon as men learned by experience whence and by what exchanges the greatest profit might be made. Originating in the use of coin, the art of getting wealth is generally thought to be chiefly concerned with it, and to be the art which produces riches and wealth; having to consider how they may be accumulated. Indeed, riches is assumed by many to be only a quantity of coin, because the arts of getting wealth and retail trade are concerned with coin. Others maintain that coined money is a mere sham, a thing not natural, but conventional only, because, if the users substitute another commodity for it, it is worthless, and because it is not useful as a means to any of the necessities of life, and, indeed, he who is rich in coin may often be in want of necessary food. But how can that be wealth of which a man may have a great abundance and yet perish with hunger, like Midas in the fable, whose insatiable prayer turned everything that was set before him into gold?

Hence men seek after a better notion of riches and of the art of getting wealth than the mere acquisition of coin, and they are right. For natural riches and the natural art of wealth-getting are a different thing; in their true form they are part of the management of a household; whereas retail trade is the art of producing wealth, not in every way, but by exchange. And it is thought to be concerned with coin; for coin is the unit of exchange and the measure or limit of it. And there is no bound to the riches which spring from this art of wealth-getting. As in the art of medicine there is no limit to the pursuit of health, and as in the other arts there is no limit to the pursuit of their several ends, for they aim at accomplishing their ends to the uttermost (but of the means there is a limit, for the end is always the limit), so, too, in this art of wealth-getting there is no limit of the end, which is riches of the spurious kind, and the acquisition of wealth. But the art of wealth-getting which consists in household management, on the other hand, has a limit; the unlimited acquisition of wealth is not its business. And, therefore, in one point of view, all riches must have a limit; nevertheless, as a matter of fact, we find the opposite to be the case; for all getters of wealth increase their hoard of coin without limit. The source of the confusion is the near connexion between the two kinds of wealth-getting; in either, the instrument is the same, although the use is different, and so they pass into one another, for each is a use of the same property, but with a difference: accumulation is the end in the one case, but there is a further end in the other. Hence some persons are led to believe that getting wealth is the object of household management, and the whole idea of their lives is that they ought either to increase their money without limit, or at any rate not to lose it.

(trans. Jowett)

*NOTE*

1 Solon, frgm. 13,71 West; in fact practising the art of getting wealth results in punishment by Zeus.

## 10 Xenophon, *Spartan Constitution* VII.1–5

Of all Greek cities, Sparta perhaps came closest to the ideal of the self-sufficient community. Xenophon describes in his *Spartan Constitution* how the laws of Lycurgus succeeded in minimizing the influence of trade and commerce.

In other states, everyone, I suppose, makes as much money as he can: one farms, another is a ship-owner, another is a merchant, and others follow trades for their living. In Sparta Lycurgus forbade the free citizens to have anything to do with making money, and ordered them to devote themselves solely to activities which ensure liberty for cities. Anyway, what need was there to worry about wealth in a society where the establishment of equal contributions to the messes and a uniform standard of living excluded the search for wealth in order to obtain luxury? They do not even need wealth for clothes, since, for them, adornment is not rich fabrics but bodily health. Money is not even to be acquired to spend on the other members of one's mess; he made working physically to help one's companions more honourable than spending money to this end, showing that the former involves the use of character, the latter of wealth. He prevented the acquiring of money by dishonesty. First, he established a currency such that even ten minas could not be brought into the house without the knowledge of the master and servants – it would take up a lot of space, and need a wagon to move it.

(trans. Moore)

### 11 Herodotus II.166–7

Greek virtue (*aretē*) was an aristocratic ideal. Warriors ranked high, traders and artisans very low. Herodotus observes that this classification was not confined to Greece alone. In Egypt and in other non-Greek countries similar distinctions were made.

I could not say for certain whether the Greeks got their ideas about trade, like so much else, from Egypt or not; the feeling is common enough, and I have observed that Thracians, Scythians, Persians, Lydians – indeed, almost all foreigners – reckon craftsmen and their descendants as lower in the social scale than people who have no connexion with manual work: only the latter, and especially those who are trained for war, do they count amongst the 'nobility'. All the Greeks have adopted this attitude, especially the Spartans; the feeling against handicraft is least strong in Corinth.

(trans. De Sélincourt)

### 12 Athenaeus XII.526d–e

These old values were not easily forgotten. In the *Deipnosophistae* (the learned banquet) of Athenaeus (third century AD), we find that the observations of Theopompus of Chios (fourth century BC) on the corrupting influences of commerce are still quoted approvingly.

Some, also, of the peoples living on the coast of Ocean are said by Theopompus in the eighth book of his *History of Philip* to have been effeminate. And again, of the Byzantians and the Calchedonians Theopompus says: 'The Byzantians had by this time long had a democratic government; also their city was situated at a trading post, and the entire populace spent their time in the market-place and by the water-side; hence they had accustomed themselves to dissipation and amours and drinking in the taverns. As for the Calchedonians, before they all came to have a share with the Byzantians in the government, they devoted themselves unceasingly to the better pursuits of life; but after they had once tasted of the democratic liberties of the Byzantians, they sank utterly into corrupt luxury, and in their daily lives, from having been the most sober and restrained, they became wine-bibbers and spend-thrifts.'

(trans. Gulick)

## II ROMAN VALUES

The Roman élite derived its income primarily from agricultural sources. Just as in Greece, this led to a value system that could find little attraction in commercial activities. A law of the third century BC that prohibited senators from actively engaging in trade was officially still in force in the third century AD. Upper-class contempt for traders and sailors found expression in philosophical discourses, was exploited in court, and found its way into works of history and biography. The early Church was no more positive in this respect. Yet, clearly the senatorial élite was not completely averse to the profits of trade. In several texts the assertion of traditional values masks the fact that members of the élite were somehow involved in business activities.

### 13 Livy XXI.63.3–4

In 219/218 BC the *Lex Claudia* was passed, which tried to curb the commercial activities of Roman senators.

He had further exasperated the Senate by the introduction of a new measure by the tribune Claudius; this measure, which Flaminius alone of the senatorial party supported, was designed to render illegal the possession by a senator, or the son of a senator, of any sea-going vessel of more than 300 amphoras' capacity, the size which was deemed sufficient for carrying the produce of an estate, any form of trade being considered beneath a senator's dignity. The proposed measure met with violent opposition and made Flaminius, who supported it, highly unpopular with the senatorial party; on the masses, however, the effect was just the opposite, and it procured for Flaminius a second consulship.

(trans. De Sélincourt)

### 14 Cicero, *II Against Verres* V.45–6

In 70 BC Cicero refers to this law in his prosecution of Verres, the corrupt governor of Sicily. He addresses Hortensius, Verres' lawyer:

Have no fear, Hortensius, of my asking what legal right a senator had to build a ship. The statutes forbidding it are ancient things, what you yourself often call 'dead letters'. There was a time when the state of public morals, there was a time when the strictness of our law-courts, ranked such an action among the most serious charges that a prosecutor could put forward. What need had you of a ship? For any official journey, vessels are provided at the public expense for your safe escort and conveyance: unofficially, you have no right to make journeys at all, nor to have property sent over sea for you from regions in which you are not allowed to own any. Why, then, in the next place, did you break the law by acquiring any such property? This would have counted heavily against you in the fine old days when strict moral standards prevailed.

(trans. Greenwood)

### 15 Paulus, *Opinions* V.28a3

The jurist Paul attests that this law was still in force in the third century:

Senators or their parents, if they are under their authority, are not allowed to collect taxes or to own ships for making profits.

### 16 Cicero, *On Duties* I.150–2

Marcus Tullius Cicero, consul in the year 63 BC, was a *homo novus*, the first member of his family to enter the Senate. It was perhaps to compensate for his background that he so ardently supported traditional senatorial values. In his philosophical discourse *De Officiis* (On Duties) he ranks different occupations, and concludes that only agriculture is a suitable activity for a gentleman.

Now the following is the gist of my understanding about trades and employments, those which free men can think of entering and those which are contemptible. First, those employments are condemned which arouse people's dislike, for example, collectors of harbour duties and money-lenders. Similarly, the work of all hired men who sell their labour and not their talents is servile and contemptible. The reason is that in their case wages actually constitute a payment for slavery. Another disreputable class includes those who buy whole lots from wholesalers to retail immediately. They would not make a profit unless they indulged in misrepresentation, and nothing is more criminal than fraud. All craftsmen work in mean trades because no one born of free parents would have anything to do with a workshop. The trades least worthy of approval are those which cater to pleasure: 'Fishmongers, butchers, cooks, poulterers, and fishermen,' as Terence says. Add to this list, if you like, perfume makers, stage dancers, and the whole musical stage.

However, those occupations which require greater knowledge or which result in more than ordinary usefulness, for example, medicine, architecture, teaching in respectable subjects: these are reputable for those whose status they suit. Commerce should be considered vulgar if it is a rather small affair. If it is extensive and well-financed, importing many products from all over the world and distributing them to many customers honestly, one should not criticize it severely. In fact, it even seems to deserve the highest respect if a merchant who has had his fill of trade, or I should say is satisfied with his profit, retires from the quayside to his farmhouse and estates, just as he sailed so many times from the sea to a harbour. Of all pursuits by which men gain their livelihood none is better than agriculture. Farming is the most pleasant livelihood, the most fruitful, and the one most worthy of a free man.

### 17 Cicero, *II Against Verres* V.167

As a lawyer, Cicero knew how to exploit the prejudices of his aristocratic audience against such lower-class activities as trade and seafaring. This comes out clearly in his attacks on Verres.

Poor men of humble birth sail across the seas to shores where they were unknown, where they find themselves among strangers, and cannot always have with them acquaintances to vouch for them.

### 18 Cicero, *II Against Verres* IV.8

One accusation was that Verres had robbed his province of works of art for his private collection. When Verres asserts that he bought these items, Cicero replies:

God help us, what a superb defence! We have given the powers and the insignia of governor to a trader, and sent him to our province to buy up all the statues and pictures, all the gold and silver plate, all the gems and ivories, and leave nothing there for anyone!

### 19 Cicero, *Letters to his Friends* XVI.9.4

Cicero's remarks about sailors, in a letter to his secretary Tiro, reveal typical upper-class assumptions about this class of men. The secretary receives the following advice before embarking for Greece:

The only other thing for me to request and beg you is not to be too hasty in taking ship. Sailors out to make money are apt to hurry things. Be cautious, my dear Tiro. You have a long difficult passage ahead. If possible, come across with Mescinius. He is not one to take chances with the sea. If not, then with some man of standing whom the *navicularius* (skipper) will respect. If you take every precaution in this respect and render yourself up to me safe and sound, I shall have all I ever want of you.

Again and again, dear Tiro, goodbye. I have written to the doctor, to Curius and to Lyso most particularly about you. Goodbye and good health to you.

### 20 Tacitus, *Annals* IV.13.2

The growth of trade during the late Republic and the Principate did not lead to a change in attitudes among upper-class writers. The historian Tacitus expresses the feeling that culture and commerce cannot be combined.

In early childhood, Gaius Gracchus[1] was taken by his father Sempronius to share his banishment in the island of Cercina. There he grew to manhood amidst landless men, destitute of all liberal arts; later he supported himself by petty trading between Africa and Sicily.

*NOTE*

1 This Gaius Gracchus was a later relative of the famous Gracchi brothers from the late second century BC.

### 21 Philostratus, *Lives of the Sophists* II.21

The sophist Proclus of Naucratis found a lucrative sideline in importing goods from Egypt. His biographer Philostratus does his best to convince the reader that although Proclus may have done business, he was certainly not a businessman.

He received direct from Egypt regular shipments of incense, ivory, myrrh, papyrus, books and all such merchandise, and sold them to dealers in such wares in Athens, but on no occasion did he show himself avid of profits, mean-spirited or a lover of gain.

### 22 Libanius, *Progymnasmata, Comparationes* (edition Foerster, vol. VIII pp. 349–51)

During the Late Empire, both pagans and Christians shared a negative view of commercial activities. The pagan orator and professor Libanius expresses his preference for agriculture and his contempt for commerce and seafaring:

Let all those who want to enjoy seafaring, let them all set sail and run risks, I prefer to praise agriculture and all those who are involved in it. If, in all seriousness, we compare these two activities, it is evident that seafaring has many terrible aspects, while agriculture contains the most beautiful things. Agriculture is the oldest activity, and was already practised by the very first people. For from the beginning they felt a need for the fruits of the earth, and in order to obtain them, they began cultivating the land. Avarice led men to sail the seas, for a desire for riches forced them to set sail and to suffer hardships. Ships were first of all used in order to raid and plunder. But also seafaring itself is dangerous, and all dangerous things must be avoided. Because seafaring is so dangerous, the sea is full of danger, but the land and agriculture are safe. What danger threatens a man who, having yoked his oxen, is ploughing the land, what risk does a man run while scattering the seed across the land? But when sailors, having weighed anchor, are leaving the harbour, they sail side by side with death, knowing that their only salvation is the wood on which they are sailing.

Fields, vines (the present of Athena), fruits, plants and crops offer the most wonderful sight, but the sea, boiling with the force of the winds, with its towering waves and frightening foam, is the very example of disaster. Rightly someone who has been rescued from all that feels that he has escaped all possible trouble.

Justice is the most beautiful thing, injustice the worst; agriculture makes people just, seafaring corrupts them. After the farmer has sown and has prayed to the gods he waits for the trees to bear fruit and for the land to yield a plentiful harvest, without doing harm to anyone. But the traders will wish to increase their possessions by misrepresentation and they can only become rich by showing contempt for the gods. They sail to every city with evil intentions, lying, misleading and cheating.

### 23 *Ecclesiasticus* 26:29–27:2

Christian attitudes towards commercial activities were not altogether different: there was the example of Jesus expelling the money-changers from the temple, and in the *Apocrypha* emphasis is placed on the moral defectiveness of merchants and pedlars.

> How hard it is for a merchant to keep clear of wrong
> or for a shopkeeper to be innocent of dishonesty!
> Many have cheated for gain;
> a money-grubber will always turn a blind eye.
> As a peg is held fast in the joint between stones,
> so dishonesty squeezes in between selling and buying.
> (*The Revised English Bible*)

**24 Ambrosius, *De Elia* 70–1**

Later, the church father Ambrose presents the greed and restlessness of merchants as incompatible with God's will:

God did not make the sea to be sailed over, but for the sake of the beauty of the element. The sea is tossed by storms; you ought, therefore, to fear it, not to use it. The innocent element does no wrong; it is man's own rashness that brings him into peril. He who never puts to sea need fear no shipwreck. The sea is given to supply you with fish to eat, not for you to endanger yourself upon it; use it for purposes of food, not for purposes of commerce. But how insatiable is the greed of merchants! The sea itself gives way to them, the ocean cannot endure their restlessness. The element is wearied with the merchants who plough their paths across it, to and fro, continually. The waves themselves are not so restless as these men; the winds themselves are not so violent as their desires. The winds have periods of rest, but the merchants' lust for gain is never given a holiday. The storm at times is still, but the merchants' voyagings never cease. Though the waters may be at peace from the hurricane, they are still churned up under the oars of the merchant ships.

(trans. Homes Dudden)

# 2 Forms of exchange in Homeric society

Self-sufficiency was the ideal in the Homeric world where the heroes were primarily landowners, but it was not always possible to achieve this ideal. The need for metal in particular, but also the need for slaves and luxury goods, could not always be met from within the *oikos*, the household. The need to look for certain goods elsewhere led to a number of alternative solutions.

### 25 Homer, *Odyssey* I.306–18

One option was to rely on the institution of gift-exchange to regulate the flow of goods between households. Relationships between aristocrats and aristocratic families were established through the reciprocal exchange of gifts and counter-gifts. Such guest-friendships also implied that later generations had a mutual obligation to exchange gifts. The rules of hospitality come out clearly from the following fragment from the Odyssey. Athena visits Ithaca in the guise of Mentes, a guest-friend of Odysseus' family. Here she meets Telemachus, Odysseus' son, who invites her to his house.

'Sir,' said the thoughtful Telemachus, 'you have spoken to me out of the kindness of your heart like a father talking to his son; and I shall never forget your words. Though you are anxious to be on your way, stay a little longer so that you can bathe and refresh yourself. Then you can go to your ship in a happy frame of mind, taking with you as a keepsake from myself something precious and beautiful, the sort of present that one gives to a guest who has become a friend.'

'No,' said the bright-eyed goddess. 'I am eager to be on my way; do not detain me now. As for the gift you kindly suggest, let me take it home with me on my way back. Make it the best you can find, and you won't lose by the exchange.'

(trans. Rieu)

### 26 Homer, *Odyssey* IV.593–608

Telemachus himself relies on a guest-friendship when he visits Nestor in Pylos. This text indicates that it was possible to ask for gifts one needed, and refuse others that were of little use. When Nestor offers horses as a farewell gift, Telemachus bluntly asks for something else.

'Son of Atreus,' the thoughtful Telemachus replied, 'do not keep me here on a lengthy visit. It is true that your tales and talks so delight me that I could easily stop with you for a year and never feel homesick for Ithaca or my parents. But my friends must already be tired of waiting for me in sacred Pylos; and now you prolong my stay. As for the gift you offer me, please make it a keepsake I can carry. Horses I will not take to Ithaca. I'd rather leave them here to grace your own stables. For your kingdom is a broad plain, where clover and galingale grow in plenty, with wheat and rye and broad-eared white barley; whereas in Ithaca there is no room for horses to run, nor any meadows at all. It is a pasture-land for goats and more attractive to my eyes than the sort of land where horses thrive. None of the islands that slope down to the sea is rich in meadows or suitable for chariots, Ithaca least of all.'

(trans. Rieu)

### 27 Homer, *Iliad* VI.224–36

It was not only the utility of the gift that mattered: the exchange also had to be balanced. In the sixth book of the Iliad Homer describes how the Greek Diomedes and the Trojan Glaucus meet before Troy, 'ready to do battle', and discover that their families are linked through ties of guest-friendship. They decide on the spot not to fight each other, and to exchange gifts:

'So now you have me as your loyal host in the heart of Argos, and I have you in Lycia, whenever I come to that country. Let us keep away from each other's spears, even in the thick of the fighting. There are many of the Trojans and their famous allies for me to kill, any of them that god sets in my way and my legs can catch: and again many Achaians for you to cut down, all those you can. And let us exchange armour with each other, so the others too can see that we are proud to claim guest-friendship from our fathers' time.'

So they spoke to each other, and they jumped down from their chariots, and took each other's hand and pledged their friendship. Then Zeus son of Kronos took Glaucus' wits away from him: he exchanged with Diomedes son of Tydeus gold armour for bronze, a hundred oxen's worth for nine.

(trans. Hammond)

## 28 Homer, *Odyssey* IX.39–47

Another option was to use force: there was only a slight difference between a just war and a raid for booty. On his long travel home from Troy, Odysseus had several opportunities to raid a foreign coast.

The same wind that wafted me from Ilium brought me to Ismarus, the city of the Cicones. I sacked this place and destroyed its menfolk. The women and the vast plunder that we took from the town we divided so that no one, as far as I could help it, should go short of his proper share. And then I said we must escape with all possible speed. But my fools of men refused. There was plenty of wine, plenty of livestock; and they kept on drinking and butchering sheep and shambling crooked-horned cattle by the shore.

(trans. Rieu)

## 29 Homer, *Iliad* XI.670–89

Cattle-raiding was also considered an acceptable activity for a young aristocrat, as is clear from Nestor's nostalgic words:

Would that I were as young, and the power was still in me, as when a quarrel arose between us and the Eleans over a cattle raid, when I killed Itymoneus, the brave son of Hypeirochos, who lived in Elis. I was driving off his herds in reprisal, and he was fighting for his cattle at the head of his men when he was hit by a spear from my hand, and fell to the ground, and his country troops scattered. Then we rounded up a huge amount of spoil from the plain – fifty herds of cattle, as many flocks of sheep, as many droves of pigs, as many ranging flocks of goats, one hundred and fifty bay horses, all of them mares, and many with foals under them. And we drove them all, through the night, into Neleus' city of Pylos: and Neleus was happy at heart that as a youngster going into battle I had met such success. Then with the showing of dawn the heralds made their clear summons for all to come who had debts owed them in holy Elis. And the leading men of Pylos gathered together and began the division of spoils – there were many owed debts by the Epeians, as we in Pylos had been weakened and reduced in numbers.

(trans. Hammond)

### 30 *Hymn to Apollo* 452–5

As a result, strangers were often approached with some caution.

Strangers, who are you? Whence come you sailing along the paths of the sea? Are you for traffic, or do you wander at random over the sea as pirates do who put their own lives to hazard and bring mischief to men of foreign parts as they roam? Why rest you so and are afraid, and do not go ashore nor stow the gear of your black ship? For that is the custom of men who live by bread, whenever they come to land in their dark ships from the main, spent with toil: at once desire for sweet food catches them about the heart.

(trans. White)

### 31 Homer, *Odyssey* VIII.159–64

Even in Homeric society the market principle was not completely absent. Trade and commerce were, however, kept at a distance from the community. As we have seen before (texts nos 2 and 3) the typical trader was a Phoenician, an outsider. The qualities needed for trading were very different from the qualities possessed by an aristocrat. It was therefore an insult when Euryalus, a Phaeacian youth, called Odysseus a trader.

Euryalus now interposed and insulted him to his face: 'You are quite right, sir. I should never have taken you for an athlete, good at any of the games men play. You are more like a skipper of a merchant crew, who spends his life on a hulking tramp, worrying about his outward freight, or keeping a sharp eye on the cargo when he comes home with his extortionate profits. No: one can see you are no athlete.'

(trans. Rieu)

### 32 Homer, *Odyssey* VIII.555–63

This is a rather surprising remark coming from a Phaeacian; after all, the Phaeacians were renowned for their seamanship.

You must also tell me where you come from, to what people and to what city you belong, so that my sentient ships may plan the right course to convey you there. For the Phaeacian ships have no helmsmen or rudders such as other craft possess. Our ships know by instinct what their crews are thinking and propose to do. They know every city, every fertile land; and hidden in mist and cloud they make their swift passage over the sea's immensities with no fear of damage and no thought of wreck.

(trans. Rieu)

# 3 Forms of exchange in archaic Greece

In the archaic period the provision of goods continued to be organized to a large extent by means other than market exchange. Piracy and plunder were perfectly acceptable means of acquisition, provided that these were directed against foreigners. In the eighth century BC the emergence of the *polis* was accompanied by a more organized form of piracy. Sometimes individuals were granted a concession for privateering. They could use this as a basis on which to build up a formidable position of power. Polycrates, the tyrant of Samos in the sixth century BC, used piracy to amass his enormous fortunes, but also to establish his power over many islands in the Aegean and over cities on the mainland. Several attempts were made to end privateering and other forms of piracy, but they were never completely eradicated.

### 33 Thucydides I.5

Thucydides describes the unorganized piracy of the days before the emergence of the *polis*:

For in early times the Hellenes and the barbarians of the coast and islands, as communication by sea became more common, were tempted to turn pirates, under the conduct of their most powerful men; the motives being to serve their own cupidity and to support the needy. They would fall upon a town unprotected by walls, and consisting of a mere collection of villages, and would plunder it; indeed, this came to be the main source of their livelihood, no disgrace being yet attached to such an achievement, but even some glory. An illustration of this is furnished by the honour with which some of the inhabitants of the continent still regard a successful marauder, and by the question we find the old poets everywhere representing the people as asking of voyagers – 'Are they pirates?' – as if those who are asked the question would have no idea of disclaiming the imputation, or their interrogators of reproaching them for it. The same rapine prevailed also by land.

(trans. Crawley)

### 34 Meiggs and Lewis 44B lines 2–14

In the fifth century BC the two cities of Cnossus and Tylissus on Crete signed a treaty in which they arranged for the division of booty from the pillage of other cities. A fragmentary inscription found in Argos informs us about the terms of this treaty.

The Tylissians may plunder the territory of the Acharnaeans, except those parts which belong to the city of the Cnossians. Whatever we both together win from the enemy, he (the Tylissian) shall in a division take a third part of everything which is taken by land, and the half of everything which is taken by sea, and the Cnossians shall keep the tenth part of whatever we seize jointly; and of the spoils both shall send the finest jointly to Delphi, and the rest both shall dedicate jointly to Ares at Cnossus. There shall be export from Cnossus to Tylissus and from Tylissus to Cnossus; but if (a Tylissian) exports goods beyond, let him pay as much as the Cnossians; and goods from Tylissus shall be exported whithersoever desired.

### 35 Meiggs and Lewis 16

In the sanctuary of Hera on Samos a statue representing a seated figure was found. The inscription tells us that it was dedicated by a certain Aeaces, who was in charge of *sulè*, a form of officially recognized seizure. There is some controversy over his identity. It has been suggested that he was the father of the later tyrant Polycrates (which implies a date of around 540 BC). Epigraphic arguments point to a later date, around 500 BC, which would imply that this Aeaces could not be connected with the tyrant's family.

Aeaces, the son of Brychon made this dedication; to Hera; he sold the revenues of the official seizure, in his capacity as president.

### 36 Herodotus III.39

We know more about the activities of Polycrates himself. Herodotus' story of the rise and fall of this sixth-century tyrant of Samos shows that his power was based on his fleet, with which he prowled around the seas.

While Cambyses was occupied with the Egyptian expedition, the Lacedaemonians made an expedition to Samos against Polycrates, the son of Aeaces. Polycrates had seized power in the island, and at the outset had divided his realm into three and gone shares with his brothers, Pantagnotus and Syloson; later, however, he killed the former, banished the latter (the younger of the two) and held the whole island himself. Once master of it, he concluded a pact of friendship with Amasis, king of Egypt, sealing it by a mutual exchange of presents. It was not long before the rapid increase of his power became the talk of Ionia and the rest of Greece. All his campaigns were victorious, his every venture a success. He had a fleet of a hundred fifty-oared galleys and a force of a thousand bowmen. His plundering raids were widespread and indiscriminate – he used to say that a friend would be more grateful if he gave him back what he had taken, than if he had never taken it. He captured many of the islands and a number of towns on the mainland as well. Amongst other successes, he defeated at sea the Lesbians, who had sent their whole fleet to the help of Miletus; the prisoners he took were forced to dig, in chains, the whole moat which surrounds the walls of Samos.

(trans. De Sélincourt)

**37 Herodotus I.69–70**

The story of Polycrates also proves the continuing importance of gift-exchange in the relationships between rulers. His friendship with the Egyptian pharaoh Amasis was confirmed through the exchange of gifts. Similarly, when the Spartans concluded a treaty with the Lydian king Croesus, they sent gifts, which, however, never reached Sardis:

This was partly in gratitude for a favour which Croesus had done them on a former occasion, when they had sent to Sardis to buy gold for a statue of Apollo (the one which now stands in the Laconian town of Thornax) and Croesus had given it to them as a free gift. For this reason, then, and also because Croesus had chosen them out of all the Greeks to be his friends, the Lacedaemonians consented to give him their help. Not only, moreover, were they ready to serve when he should call upon them, but wishing to make Croesus some return for his presents they had a bronze bowl made, large enough to hold two thousand five hundred gallons and covered with small figures round the outside of the rim. They meant to take this bowl to Croesus, but for one reason or another it never reached Sardis. The Lacedaemonians say that off Samos the islanders got wind of its presence and sailed out in their warships and stole it. But the Samians deny the theft: according to them, the Lacedaemonians who were taking the bowl to Sardis were too late, and when they heard that the city had fallen and Croesus was a prisoner, they sold it in Samos to some men who placed it as an offering in the temple of Hera. And indeed if they did sell it, it is not unlikely that on their return to Sparta they would pretend to have been robbed. So much for the story of the bowl.

(trans. De Sélincourt)

### 38 Herodotus IV.196

Anthropological studies provide us with several examples of exchange between two cultures or two societies with different economic institutions, where the exchange is carried out according to strict rules. Contact is limited to a minimal level, and is often concentrated in a specific locality. Herodotus relates how the exchange between the Carthaginians and an African tribe took place without the people involved saying a single word.

The Carthaginians also tell us that they trade with a race of men who live in a part of Libya beyond the Pillars of Heracles. On reaching this country, they unload their goods, arrange them tidily along the beach, and then, returning to their boats, raise a smoke. Seeing the smoke, the natives come down to the beach, place on the ground a certain quantity of gold in exchange for the goods, and go off again to a distance. The Carthaginians then come ashore and take a look at the gold; and if they think it represents a fair price for their wares, they collect it and go away; if, on the other hand, it seems too little, they go back aboard and wait, and the natives come and add to the gold until they are satisfied. There is perfect honesty on both sides; the Carthaginians never touch the gold until it equals in value what they have offered for sale, and the natives never touch the goods until the gold has been taken away.

(trans. De Sélincourt)

### 39 Strabo III.4.8

Another way to limit contact while enabling trade to take place is to create a special buffer, a zone or settlement where commerce can be closely supervised. Such 'ports of trade' existed in antiquity as well: traders from Massilia (Marseilles) founded a special trading-place in northern Spain where the two communities did not fully mix. Its present name, Ampurias, is derived from the Greek *emporion*, which means 'trading-place'. By the time of Strabo it had lost its original character, however, and had developed into a Greek *polis*.

Further, the whole coastline from the Pillars to Tarraco has few harbours, but from Tarraco on, all the way to Emporion, the coasts have fine harbours, and the country is fertile, both that of the Leëtanians and the Lartolaeëtans, and of other such peoples. Emporion was founded by the people of Massilia; it is about two hundred stades distant from the Pyrenees and from the common boundary between Iberia and Celtica, and this coast too, all of it, is fertile and has good harbours. Here, too, is Rhodes, a small town belonging to the Emporitans, though some say it was founded by Rhodians. Both in Rhodes and in Emporion they worship Artemis of the Ephesians, and I shall tell the reason for this in my account of Massilia. The Emporitans formerly lived on a little island off the shore, which is now called Old City, but they now live on the mainland. And their city is a double one, for it has been divided into two cities by a wall, because, in former times, the city had for neighbours some of the Indicteans, who, although they maintained a government of their own, wished, for the sake of security, to have a common wall of circumvallation with the Greeks, with the enclosure in two parts – for it has been divided by a wall through the centre; but in the course of time the two peoples united under the same constitution, which was a mixture of both Barbarian and Greek laws – a thing which has taken place in the case of many other peoples.

(trans. Jones)

### 40 Herodotus II.178–9

Other Greek ports of trade existed along the Black Sea coast, on the coast of Syria (Al-Mina on the Orontes) and in Egypt. Greek commerce with Egypt was concentrated in the settlement of Naucratis, on the Nile Delta. According to Herodotus, this settlement was granted to the Greek traders as a favour by the pharaoh Amasis (570–526 BC).

Amasis favoured the Greeks and granted them a number of privileges, of which the chief was the gift of Naucratis as a commercial headquarters for any who wished to settle in the country. He also made grants of land upon which Greek traders, who did not want to live permanently in Egypt, might erect altars and temples. Of these latter the best known and most used – and also the largest – is the Hellenium; it was built by the joint efforts of the Ionians of Chios, Teos, Phocaea, and Clazomenae, of the Dorians of Rhodes, Cnidos, Halicarnassus, and Phaselis, and of the Aeolians of Mytilene. It is to these states that the temple belongs, and it is they who have the right of appointing the officers in charge of the port. Other cities which claim a share in the Hellenium do so without any justification; the Aeginetans, however, built a temple of Zeus separately, the Samians one in honour of Hera, and the Milesians another in honour of Apollo.

In old days Naucratis was the only port in Egypt, and anyone who brought a ship into any of the other mouths of the Nile was bound to state on oath that he did so of necessity and then proceed to the Canopic mouth; should contrary winds prevent him from doing so, he had to carry his freight to Naucratis in barges all round the Delta, which shows the exclusive privilege the port enjoyed.

(trans. De Sélincourt)

When traders appear in ancient literature they normally remain anonymous. Some names have survived, however, mostly in legends. In a few texts we read about the commercial activities of historical figures in the archaic period. We know, of course, that Hesiod sailed the seas to market the produce of his land (see text no. 4).

Some of these 'merchant adventurers' belonged to the aristocracy. The landowning ideology, apparently, did not deter them from commerce.

### 41 Solon, *Fragments* XII.41–6

Solon is best known for his activities as a legislator in Athens. The story goes that, after having proposed his laws, he made the Athenians promise to stick to them for ten years. He subsequently left Athens to avoid having to change any of his laws. He travelled widely and established his reputation as one of Greece's seven sages. In the following fragment he makes some observations about the different sources of wealth.

If a man is needy and the works of poverty oppress him, he decides that he will assuredly win great wealth. Different men spend their efforts in different directions. One wanders over the sea, abundant in fish, striving to bring profit back in ships, not grudging his life, when he is borne along by the boisterous winds.

### 42 Plutarch, *Solon* II.3–III.1

Plutarch (first century AD), in his biography of Solon, holds that he as well as other aristocrats had dabbled in trade. Plutarch also mentions the reason why these activities did not diminish them in the eyes of their contemporaries.

In those earlier times, to use the words of Hesiod, 'work was no disgrace', nor did a trade bring with it social inferiority, and the calling of a merchant was actually held in honour, since it gave him familiarity with foreign parts, friendships with foreign kings, and a large experience in affairs. Some merchants were actually founders of great cities, as Protis, who was beloved by the Gauls along the Rhone, was of Marseilles. Thales is said to have engaged in trade, as well as Hippocrates the mathematician; and Plato defrayed the expenses of his sojourn in Egypt by the sale of oil.

Accordingly, if Solon's way of living was expensive and profuse, and if, in his poems, he speaks of pleasure with more freedom than becomes a philosopher, this is thought to be due to his mercantile life; he encountered many and great dangers, and sought his reward therefore in sundry luxuries and enjoyments.

(trans. Perrin)

### 43 Herodotus IV.152

The success of traders was often dependent on chance and the capacity of an individual to leap at an opportunity. This is illustrated in the story of the Greek discovery of the city of Tartessus in southern Spain (*c.* 640 BC).

In the course of their travels about Crete, the party from Thera came to Itanus, where they met a certain Corobius, a purple-fisher, who told them that he had once been blown out of his course and had fetched up at the island of Platea, just off the Libyan coast. This man they paid to return with them to Thera, and shortly afterwards a small reconnoitring party, with Corobius as pilot, set sail. They reached Platea and put Corobius ashore with enough supplies for a stated number of months, and then made sail again with all speed for home, to bring the news about the island. They had agreed with Corobius to be away a definite length of time; this period, however, was exceeded, and Corobius was in distress from lack of supplies, until a Samian vessel bound for Egypt, under the command of a man called Colaeus, was forced by the weather to run for Platea. The Samians listened to Corobius' story, left him enough food to last a year, and resumed their voyage to Egypt, which they were anxious to reach. Easterly winds, however, prevented them from getting there, and continued so long that they were driven away to the westward right through the Pillars of Heracles until, by a piece of more than human luck, they succeeded in making Tartessus. This place had not at that period been exploited, and the consequence was that the Samian merchants, on their return home, made a greater profit on their cargo than any Greeks of whom we have precise knowledge, with the exception of Sostratus of Aegina, the son of Laodamas – with him, nobody can compare. A tenth part of their profits, amounting to six talents, they spent on the manufacture of a bronze vessel, shaped like an Argive wine-bowl, with a continuous row of griffins' heads round the rim; this bowl, supported upon three kneeling figures in bronze, eleven and a half feet high, they placed as an offering in the temple of Hera.

(trans. De Sélincourt)

## 44 Strabo XVII.1.33

Strabo tells a story about Charaxus, the brother of the poetess Sappho. Charaxus traded wine between Lesbos and the port of trade Naucratis in Egypt.[1]

[This pyramid is called] 'The tomb of the courtesan', having been built by the lovers of the courtesan, whom Sappho, the Melic poetess calls Doricha, the beloved of Sappho's brother Charaxus. He was occupied with transporting Lesbian wine to Naucratis.

*NOTE*

1 The story also appears in Athenaeus XIII.596b.

## 45 B. Bravo, *Dialogues d'histoire ancienne*, 1 (1974), 123

Literary sources do not provide much information on the precise nature of the business activities of these traders. More information is supplied by a business letter of around 500 BC which was found on the island of Berezan in the Black Sea. This is a letter by (or on behalf of) a certain Achillodorus, who had apparently acted as agent for a certain Anaxagores. On a business trip a third man, Matasys, had confiscated the cargo and tried to reduce Achillodorus to slavery, apparently in order to settle some claim with Anaxagores.

O Protagoras, your father [Achillodorus] sends you this message: he is being wronged by Matasys, for he [Matasys] is enslaving him and has deprived him of his cargo. Go to Anaxagores and tell him the story, for the [Matasys] asserts that he [Achillodorus] is the slave of Anaxagores, claiming 'Anaxagores has my property, male slaves, female slaves and houses'. But he [Achillodorus] disputes it and denies that there is anything between him and Matasys, and he says that he is free and that Matasys has nothing to do with him. But as for Matasys, what is there between him and Anaxagores, they alone know. Tell this to Anaxagores and his [Achillodorus'] wife. He [Achillodorus] sends you another message: take your mother and your brothers who are among the Arbinatae to the city. But the keeper of the ship will go himself and go straight down.

On reverse:

The lead of Achillodorus addressed to his son and Anaxagores.

# 4 Athens and the Athenian empire

## I EMPIRE AND TRADE

During the fifth and fourth centuries BC trade was carried out on a regular basis throughout the Greek world. A large proportion of this trade was concentrated in Athens, which was the centre of a maritime empire.

The Delian league, founded in 478 BC as an alliance against the Persian threat, had served from the start as a vehicle for Athenian imperial ambitions. The Athenians were fully aware of the opportunities for profit which the possession of empire offered. They received tribute from their allies and confiscated land for Athenian settlers. Control over the Aegean also allowed them to monitor the flow of goods, and so secure Athenian import needs. The trade in grain was especially closely supervised (see below, pp. 94ff.), but Athens could lay claim to other goods as well. Although the Athenians could use economic power for political purposes, they were not prepared to take protectionist measures on behalf of Athenian manufacturers or merchants.

### 46 Pseudo-Xenophon, *Constitution of the Athenians* II.11–13

We do not know the author of the fifth-century *Constitution of the Athenians*. He is nowadays normally called Pseudo-Xenophon or 'the old oligarch'. It is possible that the text was written in the early days of the Peloponnesian war by an Athenian expatriate with oligarchic sympathies. He gives a perceptive, though unsympathetic, account of the workings of the Athenian state. He is fully aware of the fact that Athens uses its maritime power to secure its import needs.

They alone of Greeks and foreigners can be wealthy: where will a city rich in timber for ship-building dispose of its goods without the agreement of the rulers of the sea? If a city is wealthy in iron, copper or flax, where will it dispose of its goods without the consent of the rulers of the sea? But these are just what I need for ships – wood from one, iron from another, and copper, flax and wax from others. In addition, exports to any city hostile to us will be forbidden on pain of being barred from the sea. Although I do nothing, I have all these products of the land because of the sea, while no other city has two of them; no city has both timber and flax, but where there is an abundance of flax the ground is level and treeless, nor do copper and iron come from the same city, nor any two or three of the other products from one place but one from one city, another from another.

In addition to this, every mainland state has either a projecting headland or an offshore island or a narrow strait where it is possible for those who control the sea to put in and harm those who dwell there.

(trans. Moore)

## 47 Tod II.162

Another example of the way in which Athenians could profit from their maritime superiority to secure for themselves the supply of essential products is presented by a decree that was passed in the first part of the fourth century BC by the council and people of the island of Keos in the Cyclades. This text announced the decision to restore the Athenian monopoly of *miltos*, red ochre, which was used to paint the hulls of ships. The decree is presented as the free decision of an independent *polis* to confer a favour on a friendly nation. Yet from the style of the document, which closely followed Athenian examples, and from the terms of the decree, which give Athens not only a full monopoly, but also the right to interfere in Kean affairs to ensure this monopoly, it is clear that Athens could force its will on this little island.

Theogenes moved: be it resolved by the council and the people of Coresus, concerning the request put by the Athenian envoys, that the export of red ochre to Athens should take place as in the past. So that the decrees formerly passed by the Athenians and the Coresians about the ochre should be enforced, let it be exported on the ship designated by the Athenians and on no other ship; and let the producers pay to the ship-owners a *naullos* (transport charge) of one obol per talent. If anyone exports on another ship let him be liable to [. . .]. And let this decree be inscribed on a stone stele and placed in the sanctuary of Apollo and let the law be enforced as previously. Let information be lodged with the *astynomoi* (city-officials), and let the *astynomoi* submit the matter to a law court for adjudication within thirty days; let whoever denounces (a fraud) or gives information receive half [. . .] if the informer is a slave, if he belongs to the exporters let him be free and receive three quarters, and if he belongs to someone else, let him be free and receive [. . .]. Let there be transfer of law suits to Athens for whoever denounces (a fraud) or gives information. If the Athenians pass any other decrees on the safeguard of the ochre, let the decrees come into force from the moment of their arrival. Let the producers pay the tax of one-fiftieth to the collectors of the tax. Let the Athenians be invited to receive hospitality at the *prytaneum* (town-hall) tomorrow.

(adapted from Austin and Vidal-Naquet)

## 48 Meiggs and Lewis 45

In the latter part of the fifth century BC (440–420 BC) Athens passed a decree to impose the use of Athenian coins, weights and measures throughout its empire. Although a common currency and the unity of standards could be beneficial to traders and merchants in the Aegean, they would not be especially beneficial to Athenian traders. It is therefore not very likely that economic considerations have played a major part in this decision. The privileged position of Athenian currency and measures can more profitably be explained as a symbolic action, designed to express Athens' domination of the 'allies'.

[G]overnors [in the] cities or [. . . The] *hellenotamiai* (treasurers) [. . .] are to make a record [. . .] of any of the cities, [the man who wishes shall immediately] bring [before] *heliaia* (the law courts) of the *thesmothetai*[1] those who have acted against the law.] The *thesmothetai* shall [institute proceedings for the] denouncers of each (malefactor) [within] five [days.] If [someone other] than the governors [in] the cities does not act according to what has been decreed, whether citizen or alien, [he shall] lose his citizen rights [and his] property shall be confiscated, the goddess (Athena) receiving the [tithe. If] there are no Athenian governors, the chief magistrates [of each city shall perform all that is in the] decree. If they do not act in compliance with [what has been decreed, let there be directed against] these magistrates [prosecution at Athens] involving [loss of citizen-rights. In the] mint, [after receiving] the money, [they shall mint no] less than half and [. . .] the cities. The fee exacted [by the superintendents (of the mint) shall invariably be three] drachmas out of each *mina*. [. . .] they shall convert (the money) or [be] liable [. . . . Whatever] is left over of the money [that has been exacted shall be minted and handed over] either to the generals [or to the . . .] When it has been handed over, [. . .] and to Hephais[tus. . . . If] anyone proposes [or] puts to a vote regarding [these matters that it be permissible for foreign currency] to be used or loaned, [an accusation shall immediately be lodged against him with] the Eleven.

The [Eleven are to punish him with] death. [If] he disputes the charge, [let them bring him to court.] Heralds shall be elected by the [People . . .] one to the Islands, [one to Ionia, one to Hellespo]nt, and one to [the] Thracian [region . . . they are to] dispatch [. . .] they are to be subject (to a fine) of) ten thousand [drachmas. This] decree shall be [set up by the] governors in the cities, [after having inscribed it on a] *stele* of marble, in the marketplace of [each] city, and (the same shall be done) by the superitendents [in front] of the mint. This [the Athenians shall do] if (the peoples) themselves are not willing. The herald making the journey shall require of them (that they accomplish) all that the Athenians command. An addition shall be made to the oath of the *Boule* (council) by the Secretary of the [*Boule*, in future, as] follows: 'If someone coins money of silver in the cities and does not use [Athen]ian coins or weights or measures [but (uses instead) foreign coin] and measures and weights, [I shall exact vengeance and penalize him according to the] former decree which Clearch[us moved.' Anyone shall be allowed to turn in] the foreign money [which he possesses and to convert it in the same fashion] whenever he chooses. The city [shall give him in place of it our own coin.] Each individual (?) [shall bring] his money [to Athens and deposit it at the] mint. The superintendents, having recorded [everything yielded up by each, are to] set up [a marble stele in front of the] mint for scrutiny by whoever wishes. [They are to make a record of the total of the coin which is] foreign, keeping separate [the silver and the gold, and the total of our] money[. . .]

(trans. Fornara)

*NOTE*

1 College of six junior archons at Athens. Their functions were mostly judicial.

**49 Thucydides I.67**

Thucydides names as one of the events that triggered off the Peloponnesian Wars the decrees directed against Megara. They are often cited as an example of Athenian protectionism. In them, merchants from Megara were banned from trading in Athens and with its allies. Although they show that the Athenians were not afraid to use economic means to increase their power, their main aim seems to have been political: to humiliate and isolate Megara.

After extending the summons to any of their allies and others who might have complaints to make of Athenian aggression, the Lacedaemonians held their ordinary assembly, and invited them to speak. There were many who came forward and made their several accusations; among them the Megarians, in a long list of grievances, called special attention to the fact of their exclusion from the ports of the Athenian empire and the market of Athens, in defiance of the treaty.

(trans. Crawley)

## 50 Isocrates, *Panegyricus* 42

Athens' strong position at sea allowed it to depend increasingly on foreign countries for the supply of essential goods. Conservative observers objected to what they saw as an encroachment upon the traditional value of self-sufficiency (see text 46). Others, such as the orator Isocrates, took a more positive approach. In his panegyric on Athens, written around 380 BC, Isocrates draws attention to the fact that Piraeus is now the market of the Aegean.

[S]ince the different populations did not in any case possess a country that was self-sufficing, each lacking in some things and producing others in excess of their needs, and since they were greatly at a loss where they should dispose of their surplus and whence they should import what they lacked, in these difficulties also our city came to the rescue; for she established the Piraeus as a market in the centre of Hellas – a market of such abundance that the articles which it is difficult to get, one here, one there, from the rest of the world, all these it is easy to produce from Athens.

(trans. Norlin)

## 51 Andocides, *On the Mysteries* 133

A harbour tax of 2 per cent had to be paid on goods entering or leaving Piraeus. This tax was not collected directly by government officials, but was leased out to private tax-farmers. The following fragment of Andocides' speech *De Mysteriis* (On the Mysteries), which was delivered in 399 BC, demonstrates that this could easily lead to fraudulent activities.

I will tell you the reason for this change of front. Last year and the year before our honest Agyrrhius here was chief contractor for the two per cent customs duties. He farmed them for thirty talents, and the friends he meets under the poplar all took shares with him. You know what *they* are like; it is my belief that they met there for a double purpose: to be paid for not raising the bidding, and to take shares in taxes which have been knocked down cheap. After making a profit of six talents, they saw what a gold-mine the business was; so they combined, gave rival bidders a percentage, and again offered thirty talents. There was no competition.

(trans. Maidment)

### 52 Aristotle, *Athenian Constitution* 51

Commerce was not left unattended. The Athenians appointed several boards of officials to be in charge of different aspects of commercial activities. Aristotle mentions several of these boards in his *Athenian Constitution*.

Ten *agoranomoi* (magistrates in charge of supervision of markets) are elected by lot, five for Piraeus and five for the city. Their statutory duty is to supervise goods for sale to ensure that merchandise is pure and unadulterated. Ten *metronomoi* (inspectors of weights and measures) are similarly elected, five for the city and five for Piraeus to ensure that honest weights and measures are used by those who are selling. There used to be ten *sitophulakes* (commissioners in charge of the corn supply), elected by lot, of whom five were allocated to Piraeus and five to the city, but there are now twenty for the city and fifteen for Piraeus. They ensure first that there is no sharp practice in the selling of unprepared corn in the market, secondly that the millers should sell their barley flour at a price proportionate to that of unmilled barley, and thirdly that the bakers should sell loaves at a price corresponding to the price of wheat, and containing the full weight which the commissioners have laid down as the law requires them to do. They also elect by lot ten commissioners of trade to supervise trading and ensure that two-thirds of the corn imported is brought to the city.

## II METICS, ALIENS AND TRADE IN ATHENS

Athens' position as the political and commercial hub of a maritime empire attracted large numbers of traders. Most of these, however, were not Athenian citizens, but at best metics, resident foreigners. They were liable to taxation and even military service. Their utility to the state was recognized by writers such as Xenophon and Isocrates. Many citizens clearly had commercial interests that brought them into contact with metics and traders, yet the attitudes towards these groups were not always favourable, their privileges remained fairly limited and some reactionary observers even expressed the feeling that foreigners already enjoyed far too many privileges in Athens. Only metics who had made major contributions to the city (for example, to the grain supply) could expect some reward.

## 53 Aristophanes of Byzantium, *Fragments* 38

The Alexandrian scholar and librarian Aristophanes of Byzantium (257–180 BC) gives a precise definition of metics.

A metic is he who comes from a foreign place to live in the city; he pays taxes towards certain fixed needs of the city. For a number of days he is called a *parepidemos* (visitor) and is exempted from taxes, but if he exceeds the fixed time he becomes a metic and liable to taxation.

## 54 Demosthenes, *Against Aristocrates* 211

Metics enjoyed a higher status than other foreigners, but they still had to comply with several obligations. They were liable to a special tax, they had to find an Athenian citizen who would act as a sponsor, and they had to register in an Athenian deme. This did not put them on a par with citizens, as metics had no political rights, and were barred from the right to own land and property in Attica. Further privileges were only sparingly conferred upon them, as can be deduced from the following fragment of Demosthenes.

But the really scandalous thing is, not that our counsels are inferior to those of our ancestors, who surpassed all mankind in virtue, but that they are worse than those of all other nations. Is it not discreditable that, whereas the Aeginetans yonder, who inhabit that insignificant island, and have nothing whatever to be proud of, have never to this day given their citizenship to Lampis, the largest shipowner in Hellas, who fitted out their city and their seaport, but have reluctantly rewarded him merely with exemption from the alien-tax. . . .

(trans. Vince)

## 55 *IG* II² 207 lines 0–10

In individual cases metics received additional privileges as a reward for special services to the Athenian state (see also text no. 59).

. . . shall be *proxenos* (representative host) and benefactor of the people of Athens, both himself and his descendants, and they shall be given *isoteleia* (equality of obligations) while they live in Athens, the right to pay *eisphora* (property tax) and to pay taxes on the same terms as the Athenians and the right to perform military service with the Athenians, they shall also have the right to acquire land and a house.

### 56 Pseudo-Xenophon, *Constitution of the Athenians* I.10–12

The political pamphleteer whom we know as Pseudo-Xenophon or 'the old oligarch' argues that democracy necessarily leads to a situation where slaves and metics take too many liberties.

Slaves and metics at Athens lead a singularly undisciplined life; one may not strike them there, nor will a slave step aside for you. Let me explain the reason for this situation: if it were legal for a free man to strike a slave, a metic or a freedman, an Athenian would often have been struck under the mistaken impression that he was a slave, for the clothing of the common people there is in no way superior to that of the slaves and metics, nor is their appearance. There is also good sense behind the apparently surprising fact that they allow slaves there to live in luxury, and some of them in considerable magnificence. In a state relying on naval power it is inevitable that slaves must work for hire so that we may take profits from what they earn, and they must be allowed to go free. Where there are rich slaves it is no longer profitable for my slave to be afraid of you; in Sparta my slave would be afraid of you, but there, if your slave is afraid of me, he will probably spend some of his own money to free himself from the danger. This, then, is why in the matter of free speech we have put slaves and free men on equal terms; we have also done the same for metics and citizens because the city needs metics because of the multiplicity of her industries and for her fleet; that is why we were right to establish freedom of speech for metics as well.

(trans. Moore)

### 57 Xenophon, *Ways and Means* II.1–III.5

After the Spartan victory in the Peloponnesian War Athens lost her maritime empire. The substantial loss of income which resulted from this could only partially be compensated for by the strong position of the harbour of Piraeus. Xenophon, in his *Ways and Means*, offers some proposals to increase the income of the state. He was fully aware of the importance of metics to the revenues of the Athenians, and he makes some suggestions to increase the attraction of Athens to this category of visitors.

But instead of limiting ourselves to the blessings that may be called indigenous, suppose that, in the first place, we studied the interests of the resident aliens. For in them we have one of the very best sources of revenue, in my opinion, inasmuch as they are self-supporting and, so far from receiving payment for the many services they render to states, they contribute by paying a special tax. I think that we should study their interests sufficiently, if we relieved them of the duties that seem to impose a certain measure of disability on the resident alien without conferring any benefit on the state, and also of the obligation to serve in the infantry along with the citizens. Apart from the personal risk, it is no small thing to leave their houses and their private affairs. The state itself too would gain if the citizens served in the ranks together, and no longer found themselves in the same company with Lydians, Phrygians, Syrians, and barbarians of all sorts, of whom a large part of our alien population consists. In addition to the advantage of dispensing with the services of these men, it would be an ornament to the state that the Athenians should be thought to rely on themselves rather than on the help of foreigners in fighting their battles.

If, moreover, we granted the resident aliens the right to serve in the cavalry and various other privileges which it is proper to grant them, I think that we should find their loyalty increase and at the same time should add to the strength and greatness of the state.

Then again, since there are many vacant sites for houses within the walls, if the state allowed approved applicants to erect houses on these and granted them the freehold of the land, I think that we should find a larger and better class of persons desiring to live at Athens.

And if we appointed a board of Guardians of Aliens analogous to the Guardians of Orphans, and some kind of distinction were earmarked for guardians whose list of resident aliens was longest, that too would add to the loyalty of the aliens, and probably all without a city would covet the right of settling in Athens, and would increase our revenues.

I shall now say something of the unrivalled amenities and advantages of our city as a commercial centre.

In the first place, I presume, she possesses the finest and safest accommodation for shipping, since vessels can anchor here and ride safe at their moorings in spite of bad weather. Moreover, at most other ports merchants are compelled to ship a return cargo, because the local currency has no circulation in other states; but at Athens they have the opportunity of exchanging their cargo and exporting very many classes of goods that are in demand, or, if they do not want to ship a return cargo of goods, it is sound business to export silver; for, wherever they sell it, they are sure to make a profit on the capital invested.

If prizes were offered to the magistrates of the market for just and prompt settlement of disputes, so that sailings were not delayed, the effect would be that a far larger number of merchants would trade with us and with much greater satisfaction.

It would also be an excellent plan to reserve front seats in the theatre for merchants and shipowners, and to offer them hospitality occasionally, when the high quality of their ships and merchandise entitles them to be considered benefactors of the state. With the prospect of these honours before them they would look on us as friends and hasten to visit us to win the honour as well as the profit.

The rise in the number of residents and visitors would of course lead to a corresponding expansion of our imports and exports, of sales, rents and customs.

(trans. Marchant)

### 58 Isocrates, *On the Peace* VI.21

Isocrates, the great advocate of Hellenic unity in the face of the threat posed by Philip of Macedon, points out that unity and peace will also result in greater economic prosperity for Athens, and attract large numbers of foreign traders.

We shall see our city enjoying twice the revenues which she now receives, and filling up with traders, foreigners and metics by whom she is now deserted.

### 59 *SIG*[3] 304

Food crises were endemic in the ancient world. In the fifth and fourth centuries BC Athens was to a large extent dependent on foreign grain. In 330–329 BC Athens was hit by a particularly severe food crisis. The merchant Heraclides of Salamis in Cyprus came to the rescue of the city by selling grain below the current market price.

Proposal made by Demosthenes, son of Democles, from the Deme Lamptrae: Whereas Heraclides of Salamis (in Cyprus) has continually shown his dedication to the interests of the people of Athens and done for them benefactions to the best of his ability, and previously, during a period of scarcity of grain, he was the first of the shippers who voluntarily sold the city 3,000 *medimnoi* wheat at a price of five drachmas per measure; and then, when voluntarily contributions were being collected, he gave 3,000 drachmas to the *sitonia* (grain purchase fund); whereas he in all other respects has continually shown his goodwill and zeal towards the people, be it resolved that official commendation shall be extended to Heraclides, son of Chariclides, of Salamis, and that he receive a gold crown for his goodwill and zeal towards the people of Athens, that he and his descendants be declared *proxenos* (representatives host) and 'benefactor' of the people of Athens, that they shall also have the right of owning land and houses, subject to the limits of the law and that they have the right to perform military service and the right to pay *eisphora* (property tax) on the same terms as the Athenians. Be it further resolved that the secretary of the prytany have a record of this motion and others deriving from this inscribed on a stone stèlè and set up on the acropolis, and that the treasurer provide thirty drachmas for the inscription of the stèlè from the appropriate funds.

### 60 Tod II.189

Foreign traders in Athens and Piraeus could be united in associations that were organized on the basis of origin. The purposes of these associations were more often social and religious than purely professional. In 333 BC merchants from Citium, on Cyprus, got permission to construct in Athens a sanctuary for the goddess Isis.

In Nicocrates' archonship, when Aegeis held the first prytany. Of the *proedroi* (presiding officers of the *boule*) the one who put the question to the vote was Theophilus of Phegous. Resolved by the *boule* (council), Antidotus, son of Apollodorus, of Sypalettus made the motion: Concerning the request of the Citians regarding the foundation of the temple to Aphrodite, let it be resolved by the *boule* that the *proedroi*, whoever are chosen by lot to be *proedroi*, at the first assembly shall introduce them and transact the business, and that the opinion shall be communicated, (the opinion) of the *boule*, to the people that it seems good to the *boule* that the people, when they have heard from the Citians about the foundation of the temple and from any other of the Athenians who wishes, shall decide whatever to them seems to be best. In Nicocrates' archonship, when Pandionis held the second prytany. Of the *proedroi* the one who put the question to the vote was Phanostratus of Philaedae. Resolved by the people. Lycurgus, son of Lycophro, of Boutadae made the motion: Concerning the matters that the merchants (that is, the) Citians have decided to make a lawful supplication in requesting from the people the privilege of possession of a plot on which to build a temple of Aphrodite, let it be resolved by the people that there shall be given to the merchants from Cition the privilege of possession of a plot on which to build the temple of Aphrodite, just as also by the Egyptians the temple of Isis has been built.

(adapted from Harding)

## 61 Demosthenes, *Against Euboulides* 30–1; 33–4; 35

Traders in Piraeus and Athens were often metics and other foreigners. Yet citizens could also be involved in commercial activities. Demosthenes' speech against Euboulides of 346 BC is about citizenship. A certain Euxitheus was accused by Euboulides of posing as a citizen, without fulfilling all the necessary qualifications. Suspicion about his descent was increased by the fact that his mother sold ribbons on the market. In the following fragments Euxitheus counters the accusation, arguing that citizenship and involvement in petty trade are indeed compatible.

With regard to my mother (for they make her too a reproach against me) I will speak, and will call witnesses to support my statements. And yet, men of Athens, in reproaching us with service in the market Euboulides has acted, not only contrary to your decree, but also contrary to the laws which declare that anyone who makes business in the market a reproach against any male or female citizen shall be liable to the penalties for evil-speaking. We on our part acknowledge that we sell ribbons and do not live in the manner we could wish, and if in your eyes, Euboulides, this is a sign that we are not Athenians, I shall prove to you the very opposite – that it is not permitted to any alien to do business in the market . . . .

It seems to me certainly that our carrying on a trade in the market-place is the strongest proof that this fellow is bringing against us charges which are false. He asserts that my mother is a vendor of ribbons and that everybody has seen her. Well then, there ought to be many to testify from knowledge who she is, and not from hearsay only. If she was an alien, they ought to have examined the market-tolls, and have shown whether she paid the alien's tax, and from what country she came. . . .

And finally:

If we were rich we should not be selling ribbons nor be in want in any way. But what has this to do with our descent? Nothing whatever, in my opinion.

(trans. Vince)

## 62 Demosthenes, *Against Aristogeiton* I.50–2

Many Athenians were in one way or another involved in commercial activities. Demosthenes makes capital of this fact in his speech against the sophist Aristogeiton. He addresses a jury of Athenian citizens, raising doubts about the morality of Aristogeiton.

Just consider. There are something like 20,000 citizens in all. Every single one of them frequents the market-place on some business (you may be sure), either public or private. Not so the defendant. He cannot point to any decent or honourable business in which he has spent his life; he does not use his talents in the service of the State; he is not engaged in a profession or in agriculture or in any other business; he takes no part in any charitable or social organization: but he makes his way through the market-place like a snake or a scorpion with sting erect, darting hither and thither, on the look-out for someone on whom he can call down disaster or calumny or mischief of some sort, or whom he can terrify till he extorts money from him.

(trans. Vince)

## 63 Lysias, *Against Diogeiton* 4–7

Lysias' speech against Diogeiton accuses him of dishonesty in handling the estate of his brother Diodotus. The latter had made a fortune in maritime trade before he took off as a hoplite on campaign with Thrasyllus, during which campaign he died.

Diodotus and Diogeiton, gentlemen of the jury, were brothers born of the same father and mother, and they had divided between them the personal estate, but held the real property in partnership. When Diodotus had made a large fortune in shipping business, Diogeiton induced him to marry the one daughter that he had, and two sons and a daughter were born to him. Some time later, when Diodotus was enrolled for infantry service, he summoned his wife, who was his niece, and her father, who was also his father-in-law and his brother, and grandfather and uncle of the little ones, as he felt that owing to these connexions there was nobody more bound to act justly by his children: he then gave him a will and five talents of silver in deposit; and he also produced an account of his loans on bottomry, amounting to seven talents and forty minas . . . and two thousand drachmas invested in the Chersonese. He charged him, in case anything should happen to himself, to dower his wife and his daughter with a talent each, and to give his wife the contents of the room; he also bequeathed to his wife twenty minas and thirty staters of Cyzicus. Having made these arrangements and left duplicated deeds in his house, he went to serve abroad with Thrasyllus. He was killed at Ephesus.

(trans. Lamb)

### 64 *Digest* XLVII.22.4

Not only foreign traders joined in associations. According to the Roman lawyer Gaius it had been legal in Athens since the days of Solon to form voluntary associations for religious as well as commercial purposes.

Members are those who belong to the same association which the Greeks call *hetaireia*. They are legally authorized to make whatever agreement they may desire with one another, provided they do nothing in violation of the public law.

The enactment appears to have been taken from that of Solon, which is as follows: 'If the people, or brothers, or those who are associated together for the purpose of sacrifice, or sailors, or those who are buried in the same tomb, or members of the same society who generally live together, should have entered, or do enter into any contract with one another, whatever they agree upon shall stand, if the public laws do not forbid it.'

## III MARITIME LOANS

Productive loans were rare in the ancient world with one major exception: bottomry or maritime loans. The general principle of the maritime loan is that an *emporos* (merchant) or *naukleros* (shipowner) borrows money to pay for the cargo. The loan and the interest have to be paid back on the ship's return out of the profits made from the sale of the cargo. In case of shipwreck the debt is cancelled. This practice remained current throughout the Hellenistic and the Roman periods. In the Middle Ages it was reintroduced by Italian traders and merchants.

### 65 Demosthenes, *Against Aphobus* I.9–11

In Athens, wealthy citizens generally provided the loan: the actual trading was normally done by metics and other foreigners. These productive loans offered good opportunities for respectable citizens with a need for cash. The father of the orator Demosthenes had a considerable fortune made up of a variety of economic assets, including seventy minas worth of outstanding maritime loans made through a middleman.

My father, men of the jury, left two factories, both doing a large business. One was a sword-manufactory, employing thirty-two or thirty-three slaves, most of them worth five or six minas each and none worth less than three minas. From these my father received a clear income of thirty minas each year. The other was a sofa-manufactory, employing twenty slaves, given to my father as security for a debt of forty minas. These brought him in a clear income of twelve minas. In money he left as much as a talent, loaned at the rate of a drachma a month, the interest of which amounted to more than seven minas a year. This was the amount of productive capital which my father left, as these men will themselves admit, the principal amounting to four talents and 5,000 drachmas, and the proceeds to fifty minas each year. Besides this, he left ivory and iron, used in the factory, and wood for sofas, worth about eighty minas; and gall and copper, which he had bought for seventy minas; furthermore, a house worth 3,000 drachmas, and furniture and plate, and my mother's jewelry and apparel and ornaments, worth in all 10,000 drachmas, and in the house eighty minas in silver. To these sums left by him at home we must add seventy minas, a maritime loan through agency of Xuthus; 2,400 drachmas in the bank of Pasion, 600 in that of Pylades, 1,600 in the hands of Demomeles, son of Demon, and about a talent loaned without interest in sums of 200 or 300 drachmas. The total of these last sums amounts to more than eight talents and fifty minas, and the whole taken together you will find on examination to come to about fourteen talents.

### 66 Demosthenes, *Against Apaturius* 4–5

In spite of his fortune, the father of Demosthenes does not seem to have owned a rural estate. Most known purveyors of maritime loans were apparently not wealthy landowners, but people who were somehow engaged in commerce themselves. Androcles, one of the two partners who had provided a certain Lacritus with a maritime loan, describes himself as a merchant (Demosthenes, *Against Lacritus* 49). The plaintiff in the case against the swindler Apaturios states that he was a trader himself before he started his career as a money-lender.

I, men of the jury, have by now been for a long time engaged in foreign trade, and up to a certain time risked the sea in my own person; it is not quite seven years since I gave up voyaging, and, having a moderate capital, I try to put it to work by making loans on adventures overseas. As I have visited many places and spend my time in your exchange, I know most of those who are seafarers, and with these men from Byzantium I am on intimate terms through having myself spent much time there.

(trans. Vince)

### 67 Theophrastus, *Characters* XXVIII.1–2

On the whole, it was not done to connect oneself too overtly with maritime trade. Theophrastus parodies this in his 'boastful character'.

The boastful character will stand at the pier and tell foreigners of the large capital that he has at sea, and expand upon the great size of his money lending business, and how much he has personally gained or lost through it.

### 68 Demosthenes, *Against Lacritus* 10–13

Nearly all detailed evidence on maritime loans in Athens comes from the court-speeches of Demosthenes. Maritime loans could be fairly complex operations, which could lead to conflicts between creditors and debtors. In some cases the conflict ended in the courts. In Demosthenes' speech against Lacritus the plaintiffs quote in full the contract that they concluded with the fraudulent traders.

Androcles of Sphettus and Nausicrates of Carystus lent to Artemon and Apollodorus, both of Phaselis, 3000 drachmas in silver for a voyage from Athens to Mende or Scione, and thence to Bosporus – or if they so choose, for a voyage to the left parts of the Pontus as far as the Borysthenes, and thence back to Athens, on interest at the rate of 225 drachmas on the 1,000; but, if they should sail out from Pontus to Hieron after the rising of Arcturus, at 300 on the 1,000, on the security of 3,000 jars of wine of Mende, which shall be conveyed from Mende or Scione in the twenty-oared ship of which Hyblesius is owner. They give these goods as security, owing no money upon them to any other person, nor will they make any additional loan upon this security; and they agree to bring back to Athens in the same vessel all the goods put on board in Pontus as a return cargo; and, if the goods are brought safe to Athens, the borrowers are to pay to the lenders the money due in accordance with the agreement within twenty days after they shall have arrived at Athens, without deduction save for such jettison as the passengers shall have made by common agreement, or for money paid to enemies; but without deduction for any other loss. And they shall deliver to the lenders in their entirety the goods offered as security to be under their absolute control until such time as they shall themselves have paid the money due in accordance with the agreement. And, if they shall not pay it within the time agreed upon, it shall be lawful for the lenders to pledge the goods or even to sell them for such price as they can get; and if the proceeds fall short of the sum which the lenders should receive in accordance with the agreement, it shall be lawful for the lenders, whether severally or jointly, to collect the amount by proceeding against Artemon and Apollodorus, and against all their property whether on land or sea, wheresoever it may be, precisely as if judgement had been rendered against them and they had defaulted in payment. And, if they do not enter Pontus, but remain in the Hellespont ten days after the rising of the dog-star, and disembark their goods at a port where the Athenians have no right of reprisals, and from thence complete their voyage to Athens, let them pay the interest written into the contract the year before. And if the vessel in which the goods shall be conveyed suffers aught beyond repair, but the security is saved, let whatever is saved be the joint property of the lenders. And in regard to these matters nothing shall have greater effect than the agreement.

Witnesses: Phormio of Piraeus, Cephisodotus of Boeotia, Heliodorus of Pitthus.

(trans. Vince)

**69 Demosthenes, *Against Zenothemis* 4–6**

The provision that the maritime loan did not need to be paid back in case of shipwreck caused problems: in a number of cases the traders falsely claimed to have lost the ship. The accused in Demosthenes' speech against Zenothemis of 350 BC had scuttled their ship themselves, in order to avoid the obligation to pay back their loans.

Zenothemis, who is here before you, being an underling of Hegestratus, the shipowner, who he himself in his complaint states to have been lost at sea (how, he does not add, but I will tell you), concocted with him the following fraud. Both of them borrowed money in Syracuse. Hegestratus admitted to those lending money to Zenothemis, if inquiries were made, that there was on board the ship a large amount of grain belonging to the latter; and the plaintiff admitted to those lending money to Hegestratus that the cargo of the ship was his. As one was the shipowner and the other a passenger, they were naturally believed in what they said of one another. But immediately on getting the money, they sent it home to Massilia, and put nothing on board the ship. The agreement being, as is usual in all such cases, that the money was to be paid back if the ship reached port safely, they laid a plot to sink the ship, that so they might defraud their creditors. Hegestratus, accordingly, when they were two or three days' voyage from land, went down by night into the hold of the vessel, and began to cut a hole in the ship's bottom, while Zenothemis, as though knowing nothing about it, remained on deck with the rest of the passengers. When the noise was heard, those on the vessel saw that something wrong was going on in the hold, and rushed down to bear aid. Hegestratus, being caught in the act, and expecting to pay the penalty, took to flight, and, hotly pursued by the others, flung himself into the sea. It was dark, and he missed the ship's boat, and so was drowned. Thus, miserable as he was, he met a miserable end as he deserved, suffering the fate which he purposed to bring about for others.

(trans. Vince)

### 70 Demosthenes, *Against Phormio* 6–9

In his case against Phormio a certain Chrysippus argues that he has provided him with a maritime loan, but that Phormio has tried to con him in several ways.

I, men of Athens, lent to this man, Phormio, twenty minas for the double voyage to Pontus and back, on the security of goods of twice that value, and deposited a contract with Cittus the banker. But, although the contract required him to put on board the ship goods to the value of 4,000 drachmas, he did the most outrageous thing possible. For while still in the Piraeus he, without our knowledge, secured an additional loan of 4,500 drachmas from Theodorus the Phoenician, and one of 1,000 drachmas from Lampis the shipowner. And, whereas he was bound to purchase at Athens a cargo worth 115 minas, if he was to perform for all his creditors what was written in their agreements, he purchased only a cargo worth 5,500 drachmas, including the provisions; while his debts were seventy-five minas. This was the beginning of his fraud, men of Athens; he neither furnished security, nor put the goods on board the ship, although the agreement absolutely bade him do so.

Having arrived in Bosporus, Phormio was not able to sell his goods.

When he came, then, to Bosporus, having letters from me, which I had given him to deliver to my slave, who was spending the winter there, and to a partner of mine, in which letter I had stated the sum which I had lent and the security, and bade them, as soon as the goods should be unshipped, to inspect them and keep an eye on them, the fellow did not deliver to them the letters which he had received from me, in order that they might know nothing of what he was doing; and, finding that business in Bosporus was bad owing to the war which had broken out between Paerisades and the Scythian, and that there was no market for the goods which he had brought, he was in great perplexity; for his creditors, who had lent him money for the outward voyage, were pressing him for payment. When, therefore, the shipowner bade him put on board according to the agreement the goods bought with my money, this fellow, who now alleges that he has paid the debt in full, said that he could not ship the goods because his trash was unsaleable; and he bade him put to sea, saying that he himself would sail in another ship as soon as he should dispose of the cargo.

(trans. Vince)

Lampis' vessel was shipwrecked, however. Now Phormio claimed that his merchandise had also been on the ship, and that he was thus excused from the obligation to pay back his loan.

# 5 The Greek world outside Athens

## 71 Polybius IV.38.1–10

Athens was not the only city where maritime commerce flourished. The city of Byzantium was able, due to its strategic position at the entrance to the Black Sea, to attract foreign trade. Polybius (200–188 BC) implies that its function as a centre of redistribution was of great importance for the urban economy.

The site of Byzantium is as regards the sea more favourable to security and prosperity than that of any other city in the world known to us, but as regards the land it is most disadvantageous in both respects. For, as concerning the sea, it completely blocks the mouth of the Pontus in such a manner that no one can sail in or out without the consent of the Byzantines. So that they have complete control over the supply of all those many products furnished by the Pontus which men in general require in their daily life. For as regards necessities it is an undisputed fact that the most plentiful supplies and best qualities of cattle and slaves reach us from the countries lying round the Pontus, while among luxuries the same countries furnish us with abundance of honey, wax, and preserved fish, while of the superfluous produce of our countries they take olive-oil and every kind of wine. As for corn there is a give-and-take, they sometimes supplying us when we require it and sometimes importing it from us. The Greeks, then, would entirely lose all this commerce or it would be quite unprofitable to them, if the Byzantines were disposed to be deliberately unfriendly to them, and had made common cause formerly with the Gauls and more especially at present with the Thracians, or if they had abandoned the place altogether. For, owing to the narrowness of the strait and the numbers of the barbarians on its banks, it would evidently be impossible for our ships to sail into the Pontus. Though perhaps the Byzantines themselves are the people who derive most financial benefit from the situation of their town, since they can readily export all their superfluous produce and import whatever they require on advantageous terms and without any danger or hardship, yet, as I said, they are of great service to other peoples.

(trans. Paton)

### 72 Heraclides Creticus I.23.4–24

Similarly, but on a much smaller scale, location by the sea was important for the tiny community of Anthedon, in Boeotia on the Euboean gulf. A third-century description of Greece suggests that it depended economically on fishing, boatbuilding and maintaining ferry services. Such specialized activities make little sense in a purely local economy: the precarious existence of Anthedon depended on contacts with other communities that provided a market for the fish (not a staple food in antiquity) and the purple shells as well as for the boatbuilding and ferry activities.

From there to Anthedon is a distance of 160 stades. It is a side road, though suitable for traffic; the journey goes through fields. The city is not large; it lies on the Euboean sea and has an agora all planted with trees and enclosed by double colonnades. It has plenty of wine and fish, but is poor in grain because of the infertility of the soil. The inhabitants are almost all fishermen who make their living from hooks, fishes, and also from purple shells and sponges; they have grown old on the shore, amid the seaweed and in their huts. They have red hair and are all slim: the tips of their fingernails are worn out, as they are devoted to working at sea. The majority are ferrymen and shipbuilders; they do not cultivate the land and in fact have none to cultivate, and they say they are descended from Glaucus the seaman, who is generally agreed to have been a fisherman.

(trans. Austin)

### 73 Strabo XIV.2.5

The port of Rhodes flourished from the late fourth century BC until 167 BC when the Romans ended its independence. Its success was due to its strategic location in between the great Hellenistic kingdoms, and to the fact that the Rhodians were able to keep the seas round the island free from pirates by using fast ships with well-trained crews.

The city of the Rhodians lies on the eastern promontory of Rhodes; and it is so far superior to all others in harbours and roads and walls and improvements in general that I am unable to speak of any other city as equal to it, or even as almost equal to it, much less superior to it. It is remarkable also for its good order, and for its careful attention to the administration of affairs of state in general; and in particular to that of naval affairs, whereby it held the mastery of the sea for a long time and overthrew the business of piracy, and became a friend to the Romans and to all kings who favoured both the Romans and the Greeks. Consequently it not only has remained autonomous, but also has been adorned with many votive offerings, which for the most part are to be found in the Dionysium and the gymnasium, but partly in other places.

(trans. Jones)

### 74 Polybius XXX.31.10–12

Economically Rhodes profited from its function as a transit port mainly by levying harbour duties. In the second century BC the Romans created a free port in Delos. Polybius reports how in 170 BC a Rhodian envoy to Rome calculated the financial loss that this decision implied for Rhodes. On the assumption that Rhodes did not differ from other communities and levied a 2 per cent *ad valorem* tax, his calculations imply a yearly turnover of about 50 million drachmas.

But the greatest calamity inflicted on our town is this. The revenue we drew from our harbour has ceased owing to your having made Delos a free port, and deprived our people of that liberty by which our rights as regards our harbour and all the other rights of our city were properly guarded. It is not difficult to convince you of the truth of this. For while the harbour-dues in former times were farmed for a million drachmas, they now fetch only a 150,000, so that your displeasure, men of Rome, has only too heavily visited the vital resources of the state.

(trans. Paton)

### 75 *SEG* XI 1026

In the fourth or third century BC the authorities of Cyparissia on the west coast of the Peloponnese also levied a 2 per cent tax on goods on import and export.

God (be with us). If anyone imports into the territory of the Cyparissians, whenever he unloads the merchandise, he is to register it with the *pentekostogoi* (officials collecting a tax of a fiftieth), and pay the two per cent tax before he brings it ashore or sells it. If he fails to do so, he is to pay tenfold. Whatever someone exports by sea, having registered it with the officials, and paid the two per cent tax, he is to deposit it. If he fails to do so, he shall pay ten times the amount due in according to the agreement. If someone quotes less than the full value, the official shall impose whatever fine he wishes, in accordance with the agreement.

## 76 Strabo X.5.4

The major claim to fame of the island Delos in the Cyclades was that the goddess Leto had given birth there to her twins, Apollo and Artemis. The island could boast the presence of sanctuaries for Apollo and Leto, and the main festivals for the gods continued to attract large numbers of foreign visitors. Politically it had long been subjected to Athens, but from 314 to 167 BC it was independent. During this period it developed into an important commercial centre.

Now although Delos had become so famous, yet the raising of Corinth to the ground by the Romans increased its fame still more; for the importers changed their business to Delos because they were attracted both by the immunity which the temple enjoyed and by the convenient situation of the harbour; for it is happily situated for those who are sailing from Italy and Greece to Asia. The general festival is a kind of commercial affair, and it was frequented by Romans more than by any other people, even when Corinth was still in existence. And when the Athenians took the island they at the same time took good care of the importers as well as of the religious rites. But when the generals of Mithridates, and the tyrant who caused it to revolt, visited Delos, they completely ruined it, and when the Romans again got the island, after the king withdrew to his homeland, it was desolate; and it has remained in an impoverished condition until the present time. It is now held by the Athenians.

(trans. Jones)

## 77 *SIG*[3] 493

Delos was a small community with some 5,000 to 6,000 inhabitants. It did not have many local products to offer to foreign merchants. Delos' main function was that of a transit port. It was perhaps best known for its notorious slave market, where reputedly up to 10,000 slaves could be handled in one day (see text no. 157). Moreover, it was an important centre for oriental products and for grain. A decree of Histiaea on Euboea of 230–220 BC shows that the grain commissioners of that city were expressly sent to Delos to purchase grain.

*Side A*

(In a crown) The people of Histiaea (crowns) Athenodorus son of Pisagoras. The archons proposed that the council should submit to the people the following resolution: since Athenodorus son of Pisagoras of Rhodes continues to show his goodwill to the people and provides services privately to any citizen who is in need and publicly to the city, and (since) in every way he provided ready assistance to the *sitonai* (corn commissioners) sent by the city to Delos and lent them money without interest, and enabled them to discharge their duties as quickly as possible, preferring the good of the city to his private gain; therefore, so that all may know that the people of Histiaea knows how to honour its benefactors and more people may compete to provide benefits to the city when they see worthy men being honoured; with good fortune, be it resolved by the people, to honour Athenodorus son of Pisagoras of Rhodes for his goodwill towards the city and to crown him with an olivewreath for his excellence and his goodwill towards the people of Histiaea, to proclaim the crown at the procession of the *Antigoneia*, and that the *agonothetes*[1] shall see to the proclamation; to grant him and his descendants citizenship according to the law and precedence of access to the council and the people after sacred matters; to inscribe this decree on a stone stele and dedicate it here (i.e. in Histiaea) in the sanctuary of Dionysus and at Delos in the sanctuary of Apollo after asking the community of the Delians for a place; the expense for the inscription shall be provided by the presiding treasurer.

*Side B*

Resolved by the council and the people; Parmenion son of Polybulus moved; to grant to the Histiaeans the place in the sanctuary [which] they are requesting, between the statues of Ophell[. . . and . . .]ikis for the dedication of the stele on which are [inscribed] the honours granted by the Histiaeans to Athenodorus; Theophas son of Cleosthenes put to the vote.

(trans. Austin)

*NOTE*

1 Official responsible for putting in public games.

**78 Dio Chrysostomus VIII.9**

The connection between a religious festival and commercial activities was not peculiar to Delos. Dio Chrysostomus tells the story of the cynic philosopher Diogenes who visited the Isthmian games, where he wanted to study the behaviour of men in large gatherings. The games had not only attracted sports fans, but also hosts of artists, poets and traders (see text no. 115).

That was the time, too, when one could hear crowds of wretched sophists around Poseidon's temple shouting and reviling one another, and their disciples, as they were called, fighting with one another, many writers reading aloud their stupid works, many poets reciting their poems while others applauded them, many jugglers showing their tricks, many fortunetellers interpreting fortunes, lawyers innumerable perverting judgement, and peddlers not a few peddling whatever they happened to have.

(trans. Cohoon)

## 79 *I. Delos* 1520

As elsewhere, the foreign traders who frequented the port could be organized in associations that combined religious and national feelings with professional interests. We know of associations of traders who worshipped Apollo, Heracles and Poseidon. In 149 or 148 BC the Delian association of Poseidoniasts of Berytus (Beirut) set up an honorary decree to the Roman banker Marcus Minatius, who had lent money to the association and who had also acted as its benefactor.

[To good fortune. In the archonship of——. Resolution of the Delian] Society of Worshippers of Poseidon from Berytus, merchants and shippers and warehousemen. Inasmuch as, when the Association required funds for the completion of the chapel and for the repayment of the moneys which had been lent to it, in order that not only the resolutions passed may receive their due completion but that the others also, in view of the fair dealing of the Association, may not be hesitant to give themselves up to the interests of their societies, Marcus Minatius, son of Sextus, a Roman, being a good man and true, piously disposed towards the gods and inspired by a love of glory in his dealings with the Association, both individually and corporately, seeks glory by securing that the purpose of the Society may be safeguarded and that the chapel may be completed in accordance with the resolutions previously passed, and contributed the interest to a large amount and, after collecting the sum which he advanced as a loan, (gave this) to those who were elected to carry out the construction of the precinct, and, being consistent with himself, also made to the Society a contribution of 7,000 drachmas, and has further invited us all to the sacrifice, which he has prepared to discharge to the gods on behalf of the Association, and to the banquet, and promises that for the future also, maintaining the same attitude, he will always be responsible for some good to the Society; in order, therefore, that the Association too may make it clear that it honours those who are men of worth and never fails on any occasion in the rendering of thanks, etc.

With good fortune, the Society has resolved to praise Marcus

Minatius, son of Sextus, of Rome, and cordially to welcome the offer which he has made, seeking distinction in his relations with the Society; and that a place be granted to him in the courtyard at his own desire for the dedication of a statue, or in any other place which he himself may select with the exception of the sanctuaries and the porticoes, and in the temple whatever place he himself may wish for the dedication of a painted portrait. And upon the statue shall be inscribed 'The Society of Worshippers of Poseidon from Berytus, merchants and shippers and warehousemen, dedicated Marcus Minatius, son of Sextus, of Rome, banker, their own benefactor, in recognition of his merit and of the good-will which he continually entertained towards the Society': and there shall be the same inscription upon the painted portrait also. And let him also have a seat at the Posidea next after that of the Sacrificer, and a front seat at all the other meetings. And let a day also be celebrated in his honour each year on the day next following the procession of the Apollonia, and on this let him bring two supernumerary guests whomsoever he himself may desire. And while a golden crown, wherewith he crowned the Association, is laid upon his head, let this proclamation be made at the Posidea, 'The Society crowns with a golden crown Marcus Minatius, son of Sextus, in recognition of his merit and of the good-will which he continually entertains towards the Society, with good fortune'; and again on his own day, 'The Society crowns Marcus Minatius, son of Sextus, and also celebrates in his honour a day, both now and for all time to come, in recognition of his merit and of the good-will which he continually entertains towards the Society, with good fortune'; and in the monthly meetings, 'The Society crowns with a golden crown Marcus Minatius, son of Sextus, who is a benefactor of the Association, with good fortune'. And let the proclamations of the crowns on each occasion take place after the people. And let him also bring on the occasion of each procession one supernumerary guest. And let him also be exempted from every task and every expense. And let an ox be led in his honour every year for all time to come in the procession at the Apollonia, bearing the following inscription, 'The Society of Worshippers of Poseidon from Berytus for Marcus Minatius, son of Sextus'.

(trans. Tod)

**80 H.W. Pleket, *Epigraphica* I, no. 10**

There were several agoras on Delos, but it is quite possible that they were used mainly for social and religious activities, and that the major trading activities took place on the quays and in the storehouses along the coast, the *emporion* proper. To supervise commercial activities a board of three *agoranomoi*, market overseers, was appointed. Its functions are illustrated best by a law of 250–200 BC that regulates the trade in charcoal and wood on the island.

[No one may sell] charcoal or logs or [wood without using] the (official) measures for wood. [No one] may sell these if he has bought them on Delos, nor even if he has bought any of these [on board] ship. He may sell (these goods) only after making the (statutory) declaration in his own name. He must not sell goods (i.e. wood or charcoal) which have been publicly auctioned after bidding successfully for them, nor sell wood, logs or charcoal belonging to someone else. No one is allowed to sell except the importers themselves and they must not sell at a higher or lower price than they stated in their declaration to the *pentekostologoi* (collectors of the two per cent tax). Before selling the importers must declare to the *agoranomoi* (magistrates in charge of supervision of markets) the price stated in their declaration to the *pentekostologoi*. And if anyone sells (his goods) in violation of the regulations, he shall be fined fifty drachmas, and any citizen who wishes may bring an accusation against him before the *agoranomoi*. The *agoranomoi* shall introduce the cases before the Thirty One during the month in which the accusation was made. The accuser must pay the (statutory) deposit to the court. If (the defendant) is found guilty, he shall pay back the deposition to the accuser as well as two thirds of the prescribed fine, and (shall pay) the remaining third to the public treasury. The *agoranomoi* shall collect the fines from the defendant within ten days of his condemnation, and they may not be called to account (for their action). If they are unable (to collect the fines), they shall declare so under oath and shall hand over the defendant and his possessions to the accuser, and they shall inscribe (these facts) on the board where the other written statements are kept and shall hand it over to the council (to be deposited) in the record office.

Those who enjoy *ateleia* (freedom from taxes) (at Delos) and who import wood or logs or charcoal for sale according to the (official) measures for wood, shall declare to the *agoranomoi* the prices they intend to charge before they begin selling, and they shall not be allowed to sell (their goods) at a higher or lower price than they stated in their declaration. Should anyone contravene the regulations, the *agoranomoi* shall not provide them with scales or with measures for charcoal, and they (the importers) shall pay to the city a fee of one drachma a day for the place where they store their wood, charcoal or logs until they remove them. The *agoranomoi* shall collect the fee from them, and they may not be called to account (for their action).

(trans. Austin)

## 81 *IG* XII 5 129

*Agoranomoi* were often also responsible for the supervision of the cities' foodsupplies. In the following inscription (second century BC) from the island of Paros, a certain Cillus, son of Demetrius, is honoured for his services to the city, and especially for his activities as an *agoranomos*.

Good fortune. Resolved by the council and people; Myrmidon son of Eumenes moved: since Cillus son of Demetrius is a good [man] and a benefactor of the city; and (since) previously when he was *agoranomos* he discharged his office [well] and justly and in accordance with the [laws], for which the people awarded him fitting honours; and (since) when he was elected to the same [office] in the archonship of Gorgus he showed himself exceedingly industrious, and made every effort to ensure that the people should enjoy prosperity and abundance and be supplied with bread and barley at the lowest prices and of the highest quality, and as regards the wage labourers and their employers, he made sure that neither would be unfairly treated by compelling, in accordance with the laws, the labourers not to misbehave but to get down to work and the employers to pay their wages to the workers without having to be taken to court; and (since) he showed proper care for all the other duties of his office, avoiding no hardship, but behaving in conformity with the laws and his whole model of life and the offices he held before he was *agoranomos*; therefore, so that the people may be seen to be rendering worthy honours to those who show surpassing zeal for the people, with good fortune, be it resolved to praise Cillus son of Demetrius and to honour him with a gold crown [and] a marble statue for his merits and for the zeal which he continuously displays for the people [and] to proclaim the crown at the tragic contest during the Great Dionysia, proclaiming [the] reasons why [the] people has crowned him; the magistrates in whose term of office the Great Dionysia are next celebrated shall take care of the proclamation of the crown. And Dexiochus came forward and said he was grateful to the people for the honours voted to his father, and that he would [give] himself the money for the statue and its dedication; therefore, so that the statue should be made and placed as soon as possible in the office of the *agoranomos* wherever they wish, without disturbing [any] of the dedications, and the [decree] should be inscribed on a stone stele and [placed near] the statue, let Dexiochus see to this [as he] promises.

Dioscuri. Resolved by the council and the people; Eumenes son of Eumenes moved: since Cillus son of Demetrius has in the past constantly been a good man towards the people and has benefited in every way the city publicly and those who meet him privately, and now when he was elected polemarch and happened to be serving as priest of the Dioscuri at the sacrifice of the Theoxenia, [wishing] to make more magnificent the festival in honour of the gods [and] to have everyone sharing in the sacrificial offerings, he has come foward [to] the people and promises to give a public feast at the Theoxenia, be it resolved by the people to praise Cillus son of Demetrius for his piety to the gods and his goodwill to the people, [and] let him hold the public feast in the gymnasium.

(trans. Austin)

### 82 *IG* XII 9 1186 lines 28–9

The conceptual difference that was sometimes made between the *polis*, the political community, and the *emporion*, the commercial centre, also appears in a friendship decree between Histiaea, on Euboea, and Sinope on the Black Sea, where it is stated that:

the Sinopians who come to the *polis* and to the *emporion* of the people of Histaea and its inhabitants, shall have safety, and freedom from seizure.

### 83 Athenaeus IV.173b–c

The presence of a port with important economic activities did not lead to a change in attitude towards citizens' commercial activities. Even on Delos the élite consisted of landowners. They may have invested in maritime loans, or in commercial property (the *synoikia* that are on record in some of the Delian inscriptions) but hard evidence of the nature of their involvement is lacking. One category of inhabitants certainly profited from the constant stream of foreign visitors: the inn-keepers and shop-owners. They were so numerous that according to Athenaeus the entire population acquired the nickname of 'table dodgers', referring to their activities as waiters at the festival banquets. In the same text he also quotes a passage from Crito's comedy *The Busybody* (second century BC), to give an example of the low esteem in which the Delians were held. In the fragment, it is said of the protagonist that he

causing a Phoenician skipper, master of a mighty purse, to give up his voyage, and compelling him to bring two ships to anchor, wanted to go from Piraeus to Delos, because he had heard that that was the one place in all the world which was reputed to possess three blessings for a parasite – a market well supplied with delicacies, a throng of idlers from all parts, and the Delians the very parasites of the god.

(trans. Gulick)

Even in commercial centres such as Delos, there is little evidence for the promotion of commercial activities by the authorities. From the accounts of the *hieropoioi* (the wardens of the sanctuary of Apollo) we know that in 217 BC the city had borrowed money to establish a fund for construction works in the harbour. In 179 BC this fund was still in existence (*I. Delos* 442 A. 118 and 355.12 respectively). But even the Delians, as far as we can tell, did not go any further towards protectionism.

### 84 P. Herrmann, *Istanbuler Mitteilungen* 15 (1965), 73, 84–6

A rare example of a more protectionist attitude taken by city authorities can be found in a second-century inscription from Miletus. A certain Irenias has been sent as an envoy to the Seleucid king Antiochus IV Epiphanes. At the intercession of a sister or the wife of the king he has secured tax concessions for Milesian products.

. . . of Antiochus, and prompting her to get from her brother king Antiochus [IV Epiphanes] immunity for the people [of Miletus] for all the products of the land of Miletus that are imported into the kingdom, so, that by means of this concession, this becomes a gift that will be famous forever, and that involves an increase in the income of the city as well as of each of its private citizens; and in all cases [Irenias] did his best, in words and action, for his country – as befits a good citizen.

### 85 *SIG*³ 525

Money was widely used in the Greek world, but the economy was not yet completely monetized. People remained especially suspicious of coins with a higher nominal than intrinsic value. When in the late third century BC the city of Gortyn decided to introduce a new bronze coinage, instead of silver coins, it had to take strong measures to ensure its acceptability. The decree also shows that not all forms of exchange had entered the monetary sphere: the exchange of grain for money was prohibited.

[Gods. The following decision was taken by] the [city] after a vote with three [hundred] men being present: one must use the bronze coinage which the city has issued; one must not accept the silver obols.

If anyone accepts (the silver obols) or refuses to accept the (bronze) coinage or sells anything in exchange for grain, he shall be fined five silver staters. Information (about such cases) is to be laid before the *neotas* (the body of young men), and from the *neotas* the Seven chosen by lot shall give their verdict on oath in the agora. Whichever party wins a majority of votes shall win, and the Seven shall exact the fine from the losing party, give one half [to the winning party] and the other half [to the city].

(trans. Austin)

## 86 Athenaeus VI.232a–b

Gift-exchange, so important in the Homeric and archaic periods, persisted into later periods. When in the early fourth century BC Hiero, the tyrant of Syracuse, concluded friendship with the Corinthian Architeles, gifts were exchanged to seal the friendship.

As for Hiero of Syracuse, he desired to dedicate to the god the tripod and the Victory of refined gold; for a long time he was puzzled to know where to get it, and finally sent messengers to search for it in Greece, who at last came to Corinth, and on investigation found it in the house of the Corinthian Architeles. He had been buying up small amounts for a long time, and had a large store. Well, he sold to Hiero's agents all that they wanted, and then, filling his hand with as much as it could hold, he added that as a present to them. In return for this Hiero sent from Sicily a shipload of grain and many other gifts.

(trans. Gulick)

# 6 Egypt under the Ptolemies

## 87 Diodorus Siculus XVII.52.5

Alexandria was one of the most important commercial centres of the ancient Mediterranean (see also no. 232). In the words of the historian Diodorus Siculus (first century BC), it was

reckoned to be the first city of the civilised world, and in beauty, size and income as well as in the number of inhabitants it surpassed by far all the other cities.

## 88 *P. Hibeh* I 39

Alexandria served as a transit port for the products of the trade with the Orient, but it was most important as an outlet for the agricultural produce of Egypt itself, especially grain. This grain was the produce of land exploited directly for the king, but some grain was privately grown. Most of this reached Alexandria as tax-grain, but it could also be marketed privately. A letter of 265/4 BC authorizes the shipment of a certain amount of tax-grain from the countryside to Alexandria.

Xanthus to Euphranor, greeting. Order the measurement through Cilles to Horus on the royal barge of which the said Horus is *naukleros* (contractor) and *kubernetes* (captain), of the grain levied on the plots of Alexander, Bromenus, Nicostratus and Pausanias. And let Cilles or the *naukleros* write you a receipt and let him seal a sample, and you bring them to me. Farewell, Year 21, Thoth 10.

## 89 *C. Ord. Ptol.* 73 lines 1–8

In 50 BC Cleopatra VII and Ptolemy XII issued a decree that made it obligatory to put grain that was grown in middle Egypt on the market in Alexandria. This may have been a temporary measure in a period of food shortage in Alexandria.

By order of the King and Queen. No-one who buys grain or pulses in the districts beyond Memphis may under any pretext ship it to the Delta nor may he bring it upstream to Thebes. But everyone shall, without giving reason for suspicion, transport his grain to Alexandria, but if anyone is caught he shall be punished by death.

### 90 *P. Cairo Zen.* I 59021

The Ptolemaic authorities exercised economic control in various ways, but they do not seem to have intended to protect the interests of Egyptian merchants or manufacturers. The main purpose of the measures was to increase the royal revenues. This also formed the background for the introduction of a closed currency system. A letter of 258 BC illustrates the situation.

To Apollonius greeting from Demetrius. If you are in good health and your affairs are satisfactory, it is well. As for me, I am attending to the work as you wrote to me to do, and I have received in gold 57,000 pieces, which I minted and returned. We might have received many times as much, but as I wrote to you once before, the foreigners who come here by sea and the merchants and middlemen and others bring both their local money of unalloyed metal and the gold pentadrachmas, to be made into new money for them in accordance with the decree which orders us to receive and remint, but as Philaretus does not allow me to accept, not knowing to whom we can appeal on this subject we are compelled not to accept . . .; and the men grumble because their gold is not accepted either by the banks or by us for . . ., nor are they able to send it into the country to buy goods, but their gold, they say, is lying idle and they are suffering no little loss, having sent for it from abroad and being unable to dispose of it easily to other persons even at a reduced price. Again, all the residents in the city find it difficult to make use of their worn gold. For none of them knows to what authority he can refer and on paying something extra receive in exchange either good gold or silver. Now things being as they are at present, I see that the revenues of the king are also suffering no little damage. I have therefore written these remarks to you in order that you may be informed and, if you think fit, write to the king about the matter and tell me to whom I am to refer on this subject. For I take it to be an advantage if as much gold as possible be imported from abroad and the king's coinage be always good and new without any expense falling on him. Now as regards the way in which certain persons are treating me it is as well not to write, but as soon as you arrive you will hear . . . . And write to me about these matters so that I may act accordingly. Goodbye. Year 28, Gorpiaios 15. (Addressed) To Apollonius. (Docketed) From Demetrius.

### 91 *P. Mich. Zen.* 60

Shipping on the Nile was characterized by a three-tier organization. A distinction was made between the shipowner, the *naukleros* (contractor) and the *kubernetes* (captain), but one individual could fulfil more than one role simultaneously. The owners appear to have come from the Greek élite: sometimes they were wealthy Alexandrians, but very often they were members of the royal family.

The contractors were often also Greek, but the captains usually bore Egyptian names. The following letter of 248 BC gives us something of the practical side of such business arrangements.

To Zenon greeting from Pais. I sailed up in the boat and we are being pestered by the man who collects the twelve-drachma tax and we have not yet . . . . We brought for Artemidorus to Memphis 500 artabas of wheat from Tephi and he gave me eight drachmas, which I spent on the boat. The sailors are not inclined to sail on the terms of a third share. Inquire at home on what terms they sail for monopoly trading and you will find that they sail on a half share. Now if you approve, write to me to repair the boat; for the opportunity has come and the boat-builders are free. The boat will then find work; for at present, as she is old, no one comes to deal with us; and if you wish, you will be able to let her for hire. I myself undertake to pay you 800 drachmas for her, on condition that she will be assigned in writing to monopoly trading. Write to me then if we are to begin work, in order that I may not sit idle in the boat with two other men. For we are getting nothing and are without the necessaries of life.
Farewell.
(Address): To Zenon.
(Docket): Year 38, Phamenoth 20. Pais the captain.

### 92 *BGU* VIII 1741

Occasionally we find evidence for the existence of risk-sharing investments. In the first century BC a group of *Hippodromitai naukleroi* of Memphis, the second city of Ptolemaic Egypt, formed a trading association that had as its base the hippodrome of that city.

Dionysius to Paniscus, greetings. Here follows a copy of a letter of instruction to Heraclides, the *sitologos* (grain-official). Farewell, Year 18, month Epeiph.

To Heraclides. Here follows a copy of a dispatch order of Apollophanes, president, and Eudemus, secretary to the *Hippodromitai naukleroi* of Memphis. Following the instructions contained in that letter, load, under the supervision of Paniscus, the royal scribe, the barge of Zabdion, son of Artemidorus, which has a capacity of twelve hundred (*artabas*) [boats]. A total of twelve hundred (*artabas*) [boats]. And make sure that you get a receipt and a counter receipt for it, as is normal.

Apollophanes, the president, and Eudemus, the secretary to the *Hippodromitai naukleroi* of Memphis to Dionysius the *sungenes* (courtier) and *strategos* (governor), and in charge of the revenues, greetings and farewell. We have provided [a boat] for that part of the harvest, which we have promised the *dioiketes* to transport out of the same district . . . .

### 93 *P. Cairo Zen.* V 59823

Although there were many specialized retail traders and pedlars, the absence of specialized wholesale merchants from the sources is striking. This may be explained by the fact that very often purchases were transacted through networks of personal contacts. This practice of trade without traders is well illustrated by a letter of 253 BC from the banker Promethion to Zenon, the agent of the landowner and state official Apollonius.

Promethion to Zenon greeting. You have written to me about the wax to say that the cost per talent, including the toll at Memphis, comes to forty-four drachmas, whereas you are told that with us it costs forty drachmas. Now do not listen to the nonsense that people talk; for it is selling here at forty-eight drachmas. You will therefore oblige me by sending us as much as you can. Following your instructions I have given your agent Aegyptus 500 drachmas of silver towards the price of the wax, and the remainder, whatever it may be, I will pay immediately to whomever you tell me to. And of honey also let five metretas be procured for me. I appreciate the kindness and willingness which you always show to us, and if you yourself have any need of anything here, do not hesitate to write. Farewell. Year 33, Pharmouthi 19.

### 94 *P. Cairo Zen.* II 59240

These personal contacts were also used to pass commercial transactions as estate business. In the following fragment of a letter to Zenon by the

Alexandrian Cleonax, he asks that some mules of his may be sent down with those of Apollonius, in order to avoid the payment of tolls.

Cleonax to Zenon greetings.
Re: the mules for which I sent slaves to you, so that they might buy them for us, hand them over to you, and send them off with those of Apollonius to the estate of Apollonius in Memphis.

It would be good if you had already taken care of the matter, but if you haven't, see to it that they send them off safely with yours as if they belonged to Apollonius, to prevent their being troubled in any way with taxes. And it would be good if you had already informed us, otherwise, write to us about them to say whether they have arrived, and whether they have been sent off and what steps you have taken to let us know that they are at our disposal, and that they are safe and well. But, if they have not yet arrived, please order your men, as we have asked you to do. Farewell. Year 33, Daison 13.

# 7 Trade in the Roman world

## I ELITES AND TRADE

### 95 Plutarch, *Cato the Elder* XXI.5–6

The Roman élite was not blind to the profits that commerce could bring. Investments in shipping, in the form of maritime loans, could be very profitable. Our earliest piece of evidence is also the most telling, as it concerns none other than Marcus Porcius Cato, the *censor* (234–149 BC). He was known as a fervent supporter of traditional Roman values. He even published an agricultural manual. Yet, according to his biographer Plutarch, he was also involved in perhaps less respectable commercial activities.

When he began to devote himself more energetically to making money, he came to regard agriculture as a pastime rather than as a source of income, and he invested his capital in solid enterprises which involved the minimum of risk. He bought up ponds, hot springs, land devoted to producing fuller's earth, pitch factories, and estates which were rich in pasture-land or forest. All these undertakings brought in large profits and could not, to use his own phrase, be ruined by the whims of Jupiter. He also used to lend money in what is surely the most disreputable form of speculation, that is the underwriting of ships. Those who wished to borrow money from him were obliged to form a large association, and when this reached the number of fifty, representing as many ships, he would take one share in the company. His interests were looked after by Quintio, one of his freedmen, who used to accompany Cato's clients on their voyages and transact their business. In this way he drew a handsome profit, while at the same time spreading his risk and never venturing more than a fraction of his capital.

He would also lend money to any of his slaves who wished it. They used these sums to buy young slaves, and after training them and teaching them a trade for a year at Cato's expense, they would sell them again. Often Cato would keep these boys for himself, and he would then credit to the slave the price offered by the highest bidder. He tried to encourage his son to imitate these methods, and told him that to diminish one's capital was something that might be expected of a widow, but not of a man. But he certainly went too far when he ventured once to declare that the man who deserved the highest praise, indeed who should be honoured almost as a god, was the one who at the end of his life was found to have added to his property more than he had inherited.

(trans. Scott-Kilvert)

### 96 Plautus, *The Merchant* 64–74

The comedy *Mercator* (The Merchant) by Plautus (*c.* 251–184 BC) is an adaptation of a work by the Greek poet Philemon. It may still serve as an illustration of Roman practices. The story is about a father and a son, and of the infatuation of the father with a slave girl owned by his son. In the following fragment Charinus, the son, tells how his father first became involved in business.

Work on the farm, dirty work and plenty of it, that was his training, and there was no visiting the city for him, except once every four years,[1] and just as he had set eyes on the sacred robe,[2] his father used to pack him off post haste to the farm again. And there he was the best labourer of them all by far, and his father would say: 'It is for yourself you plough, for yourself you harrow, for yourself you sow, yes, and for yourself you reap, and for yourself, finally, that labour will engender joy.' After life had left his father's body, he had sold the farm and with the money bought a ship of fifteen tons burden and marketed his cargoes of merchandise everywhere, till he had at length acquired the wealth which he then possessed. I ought to do the same, if I were what I ought to be.

(trans. Nixon)

*NOTES*

1 For the Panathenaic festival.
2 Presented to Athena.

### 97 Pliny, *Letters* III.19

The wealth of another senator, Pliny the Younger (*c.* AD 61–112), consisted mainly of land, but he also had other sources of income. It was perfectly acceptable for a senator to lend out money.

You will want to know if I can easily raise this three million. It is true that nearly all my capital is in land, but I have some outstanding loans and it will not be difficult to borrow.

### 98 *Historia Augusta, Pertinax* III.1–4

Literary sources do not normally provide us with detailed information concerning the commercial interests of senators. Where such information does occur, it is usually meant to damage someone's reputation. In a rather unreliable biography it was said of the emperor Pertinax, the son of a freedman who had been engaged in the wool trade, that as a senator he continued his father's business:

Up to the Syrian command Pertinax preserved his honesty. After Marcus' death he became eager for money, and for this he was attacked in remarks from the people . . . . Immediately thereafter he was ordered by Perennis (the praetorian prefect of Commodus) to withdraw to Liguria, to his father's villa; for his father had kept a cloth maker's shop in Liguria. After coming there he bought up a lot of land, and surrounded his father's shop – which remained in its original form – with countless buildings. He was there for three years and traded through his slaves.

(trans. Birley)

### 99 Dio Chrysostomus VII.104

The urban élites of the Roman Empire shared the land-owning ideology of the Roman senators. Yet, just as a Cato could be involved in commercial activities, so could local councillors. That it was possible to be *honestus* (honourable) and have commercial interests is demonstrated by a passage in Dio Chrysostomus' seventh, or Euboean, discourse. Here he discusses how rich and poor can live a decent life.

Well then, it would now be our duty to consider the life and occupations of poor men who live in the capital or some other city, and see by what routine of life and what pursuits they will be able to live a really good life, one not inferior to that of men who lend out money at high rates of interest, and understand well the calculations of days and months, nor to that of those who own large tenement houses and ships and slaves in great numbers.

(adapted from Cohoon)

## 100 *SEG* XVII 828

It was rare even for councillors to identify themselves as businessmen. The epitaph of the councillor-shipowner from Nicomedia, Telesphorus, is one of the few examples where business activities are explicitly mentioned. This and the fact that he does not mention any magistracies suggest that he belonged to the lower echelons of the local council.

Telesphorus, councillor and shipowner. For himself and for Faustina and for his children and for no one else.

## 101 *SIG*³ 838

In Ephesus, which was an important port, a mere *naukleros* was normally not acceptable as a councillor: a certain Lucius Erastus had to rely on the recommendation of the emperor Hadrian, who was also prepared to pay his entrance-fee for him, so that he could enter the council of Ephesus.

The Emperor Caesar Trajanus Hadrianus Augustus, son of the deified Parthicus, grandson of the deified Nerva, *pontifex maximus*, holding tribunician power for the thirteenth year, consul three times, father of the country, to the magistrates and the city council of Ephesus. Greetings. L. Erastus is, according to him, citizen of your city, has often sailed the seas, and has to the best of his ability been useful for his hometown. He has specialised in transporting dignitaries and has twice sailed with me, the first time while travelling from Ephesus to Rhodes, the second time when visiting you from Eleusis. He wants to become a member of the council. I leave to you the examination of his background. If nothing stands in the way and if he is worthy of this honour, I am willing to pay the money, that councillors have to pay at their entrance. Good Luck.

## 102 Lucian, *The Ship* 13

Lucian's dialogue *Navigium* (The Ship) describes a certain Adimantus, an Athenian of noble descent, who visits a large corn freighter in the harbour of Piraeus (see text no. 198). When he hears how profitable shipowning can be, his imagination starts running away with him:

I measured the dimensions of the anchors when you went off somewhere. At the same time I looked at everything and asked one of the sailors how much profit the ship brought in to its owner in a year. 'Twelve attic talents at least,' he replied. Then I went back on shore and day-dreamed of what a happy life I should have had, if, of a sudden, some god had made the ship mine: I would have built myself a house on an excellent spot, not far from the *Stoa Poikilè*, and would have left my family house near the Ilyssus: and I would have indulged in slaves, clothes, carriages and horses.

## II FREEDMEN AND COMMERCE

Trade in the Roman world was normally not carried out by members of the upper classes. Traders were usually of low status: freedmen and even slaves. As we have seen above (texts nos 95 and 98), dependent freedmen and slaves may have acted as front-men, protecting the interests of the real, upper-class, investors. Yet we should not look for a patron behind every freedman involved in commerce. Many freedmen no longer had a patron, because they were released by testament, or because they managed to sever their ties with him in other ways.

### 103 *ILS* 7029

Quintus Capito Probatus, whose tomb was found in Lyon, does not seem to have had a patron; he even acted as a patron to his own freedmen. Probatus had been engaged in maritime trade between Italy and Gaul. Apparently he had been so successful that he reached the zenith of a freedman's career: he was elected to the college *seviri augustales*, the six men who were responsible for the emperor's cult, in not one but two towns.

To the departed Spirits of Quintus Capitonius Probatus the elder, of the city of Rome, *sevir augustalis* in Lyon and in Puteoli, seagoing *navicularius* (maritime trader). His freedmen Nereus and Palaemon for their patron. He had built this tomb in his lifetime for himself and his descendants and dedicated it under the sign of the *ascia* (mason's trowel).

### 104 Petronius, *Satyricon* 76

The most famous of all Roman freedman traders is the fictitious character Trimalchio. He is a figure in the novel *Satyricon* by the Roman courtier Petronius, who wrote during the reign of Nero. The novel has not survived intact; the longest surviving fragment describes a dinner party, at the home of an absurd freedman, Trimalchio. He describes his life story, how he arrived in Italy as a little slave and how he became the darling of his mistress and his master. From then on his life was a success.

However, as I'd started to say, it was my shrewd way with money that got me my present position. I came from Asia as big as this candlestick. In fact, every day I used to measure myself against it, and to get some whiskers round my beak quicker, I used to oil my lips from the lamp. Still, for fourteen years I was the old boy's fancy. And there's nothing wrong if the boss wants it. But I did all right by the old girl too. You know what I mean – I don't say anything, because I'm not the boasting sort.

Well, as heaven will have it, I became the boss in the house, and the old boy, you see, couldn't think of anyone but me. That's about it – he made me co-heir with the Emperor and I got a senator's fortune. But nobody gets enough, never. I wanted to go into business. Not to make a long story of it, I built five ships, I loaded them with wine – it was absolute gold at the time – and I sent them to Rome. You'd have thought I ordered it – every single ship was wrecked. That's fact, not fable! In one single day Neptune swallowed up thirty million. Do you think I gave up? This loss honestly wasn't more than a flea-bite to me – it was as if nothing had happened. I built more boats, bigger and better and luckier, so nobody could say I wasn't a man of courage. You know, the greater the ship, the greater the confidence. Loaded them again – with wine, bacon, beans, perfumes and slaves. At this point Fortunata did the decent thing, because she sold off all her gold trinkets, all her clothes, and put ten thousand in gold pieces in my hand. This was the yeast my fortune needed to rise. What heaven wants, soon happens. In one voyage I carved out a round ten million. I immediately bought back all my old master's estates. I built a house, I invested in slaves, and I bought up the horse trade. Whatever I touched grew like a honeycomb. Once I had more than the whole country, then down tools! I retired from business and began advancing loans through freedmen.

Actually I was tired of trading on my own account, but it was an astrologer who convinced me. He happened to come to our colony, a sort of Greek, Serapa by name, and he could have told heaven itself what to do. He even told me things I'd forgotten. He went through everything for me from A to Z. He knew me inside out – the only thing he didn't tell me was what I ate for dinner the day before. You'd have thought he'd never left my side.

(trans. Sullivan)

## III ASSOCIATIONS OF TRADERS

### 105 *P. Mich.* V 245

Roman traders (like Roman craftsmen) were often organized in voluntary associations called *collegia*. The epigraphic evidence, which consists largely of funerary and honorary inscriptions, shows that social and religious activities were an important part of collegiate life. Membership of a *collegium* and participation in its rituals gave the individual traders, whether freedmen or freeborn, a sense of identity and a certain status in the urban community.

It is much less common to find evidence for the economic activities of *collegia*. One rare exception is formed by the statutes of an association of salt merchants, which was active in the first century AD in the Egyptian village of Tebtynis. The regulations deal with the allocation of trade areas to the individual members, who had apparently acquired a collective monopoly of the sale of *gypsum* (plaster). Apparently they were also prepared to act as a cartel, when dealing with outsiders. A striking element is the casual juxtaposition of the economic clauses with regulations dealing with the banquets and celebrations. To the minds of the merchants the social and religious activities and the economic activities did not belong to separate spheres.

The seventh year of Tiberius Claudius Caesar Augustus Germanicus Imperator (AD 47), the twenty-fifth of the month Kaisareios. The undersigned men, salt merchants of Tebtynis, meeting together have decided by common consent to elect one of their number, a good man, Apynchis, son of Orseus, both supervisor and collector of the public taxes for the coming eighth year of Tiberius Claudius Caesar Augustus Germanicus Imperator, the said Apynchis to pay in all the public taxes for the same trade for the same coming year, and [they have decided] that all alike shall sell salt in the aforesaid village of Tebtynis, and that Orseus alone has obtained by lot the sole right to sell *gypsum* in the aforesaid village of Tebtynis and in the adjacent villages, for which he shall pay, apart from the share of the public taxes which falls to him, an additional sixty-six drachmas in silver; and that the said Orseus has likewise obtained by lot Kerkesis, alone to sell salt therein, for which he shall likewise pay an additional eight drachmas in silver. And that Harmiusis also called Belles, son of Harmiusis, has obtained by lot the sole right to sell salt and *gypsum* in the village of Tristomou also called Boukolou, for which he shall contribute, apart from the share of the public taxes which falls to him, five additional drachmas in silver; upon condition that they shall sell the good salt at the rate of two and one-half obols, the light salt at two obols, and the lighter salt at one and one-half obols, by our measure or that of the warehouse. And if anyone shall sell at a lower price than these, let him be fined eight drachmas in silver for the common fund and the same for the public treasury; and if any one of them shall be found to have sold more than a stater's worth of salt to a merchant, let him be fined eight drachmas in silver for the common fund and the same for the public treasury; but if the merchant shall intend to buy more than four drachmas worth, all must sell to him jointly. And if anyone shall bring in *gypsum* and shall intend to sell it outside, it must be left on the premises of Orseus, son of Harmiusis, until he takes it outside, and sells it. It is a condition that they shall drink regularly on the twenty-fifth of each month each one *chous* of beer . . . in the village one drachma, outside four drachmas, and in the metropolis eight drachmas. But if anyone is in default and fails to satisfy any of the public obligations, or any of the claims that shall be made against him, it shall be permissible for the same Apynchis to arrest him in the main street or in his house or in the field, and to hand him over as aforesaid.

The grain supply of the city of Rome was one of the main concerns of the Roman authorities, and also one of the few economic areas where they actively interfered. The Roman state exercised direct control over grain production (especially in Egypt) and collection (as tax grain) and also over the distribution in Rome. Yet the role of the state in the transport of grain was much more limited. There was no state merchant fleet to transport grain, but the state commissioned commercial entrepreneurs. Despite the profitability of the grain trade it often proved necessary to woo the private shipowners by offering them special benefits and privileges.

### 106 *Digest* L.6.5.3–6

It was increasingly common not to charge individual traders with this task, but to leave it to the *corpora naviculariorum*, the associations of shipowners, whose members were also entitled to several privileges. The situation in the second century AD is described in a text of the Digests.

Traders, who assist in furnishing provisions to the city, as well as shipowners, who service the grain supply of the city, will obtain exemption from compulsory public services, as long as they are engaged in activity of this sort; for it has very properly been decided that the risks which they incur should be suitably recompensed or rather encouraged, so that those who perform such public duties outside their own country with risk and labour should be exempt from annoyances and expenses at home; as it may even be said, without incorrectness, that they are absent on business for the government when they serve the grain supply for the city.

A certain specific character is given to the exemption granted to the shipowners, which exemption they alone possess; for it does not extend either to their children or to their freedmen.

The deified Hadrian stated in a rescript that only those owners of maritime vessels who serve the grain supply of the city should possess exemption.

Although anyone may belong to the association of shipowners, if he has neither a ship, nor vessels, nor anything else which is provided for by the imperial enactments, he cannot avail himself of the privilege granted to shipowners; and the deified brothers[1] stated the following in a rescript: 'There are some persons who claim that they are exempt, under the pretext of transporting grain and oil by sea, for the benefit of the Roman people, but who are not engaged in maritime traffic, and have not the greater portion of their property invested in maritime business and commodities. They shall be deprived of exemption.'

*NOTE*

1 Marcus Aurelius and Lucius Verus.

## 107 *CIL* III 14165

Corporations of *navicularii* (shipowners) had originated as voluntary associations, but over the centuries, the authorities had increased their hold over them, and in the Later Empire they had developed into state agencies. Yet the relationship between the state and the associations was not only to the advantage of the state. The dependence of the state on the corporations of shipowners, for the transport of supplies to Rome and the armies, gave the corporations a hold over the government. A third-century inscription from Beirut contains a letter from the prefect of the grain supply to five corporations of seagoing merchants in Arles, in southern Gaul.

The entire case cannot be reconstructed, but this much is clear: the *navicularii* of Arles had joined forces in a conflict with the government, and had threatened to withdraw from business, if their demands were not met.

Claudius Julianus to the *navicularii marini* (marine shippers) of the five *corpora* (associations) of Arles, greetings! What I wrote, after reading your decree, to . . . a . . . s . . ., *vir egregius procurator* of the Augusti, I have ordered, and I want it to be added (thereafter). Fortunate people, may you prosper! Copy of the letter (from (J)ulianus to the *procurator*). I have added a copy of the decree of the *navicularii marini* of Arles belonging to the five *corpora* and likewise (a copy) of the documents from the courtcase conducted before me. And should the same dispute continue further, and the other (*navicularii*) appeal to justice with what amounts to a formal complaint that they will soon cease to comply with their obligations, and if the injustice continues, I request that provision be made for both a guarantee against fiscal loss in the books and for exoneration of the people providing services for the *annona*, and that you order the marking of the iron bars,[1] and that escorts from your staff be provided, who will hand over (details of) the cargo weight that they 'have taken on board'.

*NOTE*

1 These iron bars either served as fastenings of the cargo, or as an indelible scale attached to the innerside of the ship.

## IV THE AUTHORITIES AND TRADE

The Roman authorities were generally not very concerned with trade and commerce and did not pursue an economic policy to protect the interests of Roman manufacturers or merchants. The interest of the state was mainly limited to the grain supply of the city of Rome and the armies, and to the income that it received from the *portoria* (tolls), and other indirect taxes which traders had to pay on their merchandise. For most goods the duties varied between 2 and 5 per cent of the value, but for luxury goods that were imported from the Orient into Egypt, a tax of 25 per cent was due.

### 108 *P. Lond.* inv. 1562 verso[1]

Tolls were levied at the boundaries of the Empire, in the larger ports and at the boundaries between the provinces, but also in smaller cities. A second-century papyrus from Oxyrhynchus presents us with the rates of the market tax of that city.

Twentieth year
From Sarapion the younger, son of Sarapion, and Pasion son of Sarapion, the two (from) the city of the Oxyrhynchi, supervisors of the tax concessions of the Serapeum for the past twentieth year of Hadrian Caesar the lord. (AD 136/7)

Account (of receipts taken within the year?) for dealings which relate to the tax concession from Toth first to Epagomenae fifth, including the fifth. Viz:-

The tariff of the market (or market administration) of the Serapeum (is) in the hieratic category, in respect of which it is specified that through the *gymnasiarchs* (officials responsible for maintenance of the gymnasium) of each year there are collected and exacted:-

| | |
|---|---|
| From the bakers of fine bread, for each establishment | 24 drachmas |
| From bakers (or 'sellers') of coarse bread | 12 drachmas |
| From rush sellers | |
| And wood sellers | |
| And fruit growers (?) | 6 drachmas |
| From olive sellers | 6 drachmas (?) |
| From garland plaiters | 12 drachmas |
| From vegetable sellers, for the guild | 108 drachmas |
| From crop buyers | 30 drachmas (?) |
| From wool merchants | 44 drachmas |
| From grain dealers | 40 drachmas |
| From clothes makers | 4 drachmas |
| From shoemakers (?), shepherds(?), likewise for the guild | 4 drachmas |
| From tinsmiths, likewise | 20 drachmas |
| From makers (or 'sellers') of yarn, for each man | 6 drachmas |
| And from private persons (?) selling throughout the city on each stater | 1/2 obol |
| From butchers, for the guild | 12 drachmas |
| From brothels, for each establishment, monthly | . . . |
| And from those who import and sell: | |
| For olives and dates and cucumbers and marrows and vegetables, for each bundle (?) | 7 drachmas |
| For spices and beans | 7 drachmas |
| For natron, for 100 artabas | 6 drachmas |
| For rock-salt (?), for each boat load (?) | 2 drachmas |
| For pottery and green fodder import (?) | 1 drachma |
| For wood import (?), likewise | 2 drachma |
| For dung and cowpats and . . ., likewise | 2 drachmas |
| For dates, for each basket | . . . |
| Thus far the tariff | |

(trans. Rea)

## *NOTE*

1 Published and translated by J. Rea, '*P. Lond.* inv. 1562 verso: Market taxes in Oxyrhynchus', *ZPE* 46 (1982), 191–209.

## 109 H. Engelmann and D. Knibbe, *Epigraphica Anatolica* 14 (1989), par. 1–9 and 25[1]

Excavations in Ephesus have brought to light a long inscription from the first century AD, which is a revised version of a customs law for the Roman province of Asia, first issued in the first century BC. This law contains information about the boundaries of the tax district, the location of the customs offices and the rights and the duties of the tax farmers, as well as regulations about procedures and about the level of taxation.

The customs' law of Asia, for import and export over land and by sea [. . . For those coming from places] of Cappadocia, Galatia and Bithynia, which surround Asia.

Territories belonging to Calchedon and Byzantium, [which are or will be within the boundaries constituted by the mouth of the Black Sea are to pay tax] before importing or exporting by sea at the mouth of the Black Sea, at those places, where by a decree of the Senate, or by law, [or by plebiscite of the people it has been agreed and] enjoined that a customs collecting point be leased to a tax farmer. At those places everything being imported or exported [. . . .]

Similarly, for everything conveyed, driven, or transported outwards over land, the two and a half per cent tax is to be paid to the tax farmer.

For male and female slave children, no one shall be liable to pay more than five *denarii* a head.

[Whatever anyone intends to export into Pontus,] he is to declare and register with the tax farmer or his agent, before sailing past the city of Calchedon.

[Whatever anyone intends to import from Pontus into our Empire], he is to declare and register with the tax farmer or his agent, before sailing past the city of Calchedon.

[Whatever anyone is importing or exporting by sea, he is not to] divert the boat, and whatever he is carrying away or exporting to other places he is not to divert to other places in order to [evade tax; if anyone] acts [to the contrary], he is liable under the law in exactly the same way, as if he was carrying undeclared goods.

(If anyone is importing by sea or over land he is to pay import tax). If someone has once paid [this tax to the tax farmer or his agent for something] that he imports [by sea or over land], the same man is [not liable to pay the same tax] to the same [tax farmer] on the same item, a second time in the same year, provided he remains within the Black Sea.

If anyone is exporting by sea or over land, he is to pay the export tax. If someone has once paid this tax to the farmer [. . .] the same man [is not liable to pay export tax] on the same item a second time in the same year to the same tax farmer [. . .], provided that he remains outside the Black Sea.

If anyone handles fresh purple shells from the sea, he is to pay a tax of five per cent.

[No one is to remove] merchandise from a ship [with malice aforethought, nor] remove it [undeclared] with the purpose of evading taxes. If someone contravenes this rule, the merchandise and the goods [shall belong to the tax farmer; only when the tax has been paid, is the purchaser] to import or export them.

If anyone imports or exports goods by sea, he is to register them with the tax farmer [at the places mentioned below: Hieron in] Pontus, Calchedon, Dascylium, Apollonia at the mouth of the Rhyndacus, Cyzicus, Priapu, Parium, Lampsacus, [Abydus, Dardanus, Sigeium, Alexandria, Hamaxitus, As]sus, Gargara, Poroselene, Antandrus, Astyra, Adramyttium, Atarneus, Pitane, Elaea, Myrina, Old [Cyme, now Caesarea-Cyme, Phocaea, Erythrae, Smyrna, C]olophon, Teos, Ephesus, Priene at the mouth of the Maeander, Miletus, Iasus, Bargylia, Ceramus, [Halicarnassus, Myndus, Cnidus, Physcus, Caunus, Attaleia, Aspendus], Perge, Magydus, Phaselis, Side and Coryphe.

. . . On the following items there shall be no tax; no one is liable to pay tax for whatever he carries on behalf of the people of Rome; nor for whatever he transports or conveys for religious purposes; nor for public purposes of the people of Rome; nor for whatever anyone carries or sends [for personal use on a specific occasion, nor for whatever provisions anyone has for that journey, carried in good faith; nor for any public property [. . .] of the people of Rome which is carried publicly; nor for coined gold and silver; nor for money which has been counted exactly; nor for what is bought or sold for the boat and its equipment. No one is to pay taxes for slaves and domestic animals, which he brings from home, or conveys for personal use on that journey; nor for books, writing tablets, letters and documents; nor for footwear and seal rings which people use customarily while abroad, apart from [. . .] these things with which people feed themselves.

## *NOTE*

1 'Das Zollgesetz der Provinz Asia. Eine neue Inschrift aus Ephesos'.

### 110 *Theodosian Code* XIII.1.4

In the Later Empire, trade was subjected to a special tax, the *collatio lustralis*. This tax did not apply equally to all levels of the population: exemption was granted to certain categories of clergymen, and to persons involved in imperial services. Councillors were allowed to ship the produce of their own estates without being taxed, but they also had to pay the *collatio lustralis* when they were involved in trading activities. The result of this law may have been that they presented commercial transactions as estate business, in order to escape the tax.

The municipal councils shall be exempt from payment of the tax payable in gold and silver which is levied upon tradesmen, unless perchance it should be proved that a decurion is engaged in merchandising to any extent.

### 111 Pollux, *Onomasticon* IX.30–1

Customs officials and tax farmers were an obvious butt for the insults of traders and travellers: in the *Onomasticon* of the scholar Pollux (second century AD) we even find a special list of useful little words for when you wanted to insult a customs official.

Should you wish to abuse a tax farmer, you might try saying: burden, pack-animal, garotter, sneak-thief, shark, hurricane, oppressor of the down-trodden, inhuman, nail in my coffin, insatiable, immoderate, Shylock, violator, strangler, crusher, highwayman, strip-Jack-naked, snatcher, thief, overcharger, reckless, shameless, unblushing, pain in the neck, savage, wild, inhospitable, brute, dead weight, obstacle, heart of stone, flotsam, pariah, and all the other vile terms you can find to apply to someone's character.

## V THE CITY OF ROME AND THE PROVINCES

### 112 Aelius Aristides, *To Rome* 10–13

The demand of the city of Rome, with its estimated one million inhabitants, for grain and other goods was huge. The court, the senatorial and equestrian élite, and other wealthy groups provided a market for the most exotic and luxurious products. The aggregate demand of the rest of the population, not only for grain but also for other goods (such as clothing), was so large that it could not be met from Italian sources alone. The market of Rome had to be supplied from all parts of the Empire, as was realized by the second-century writer Aelius Aristides in his eulogy of Rome.

No marine rocks and no Chelidonian and Cyanean islands define your empire, nor the day's ride of a horse to the sea, nor do you rule within fixed boundaries, nor does another prescribe the limit of your power. But the sea is drawn as a kind of belt without distinction through the middle of the inhabited world and your empire. About the sea the continents lie 'vast and vastly spread', ever supplying you with products from those regions. Here is brought from every land and sea all the crops of the seasons and the produce of each land, river, lake, as well as of the arts of the Greeks and barbarians, so that if someone should wish to view all these things, he must either see them by travelling over the whole world or be in this city. It cannot be otherwise than that there always be here an abundance of all that grows and is manufactured among each people. So many merchant ships arrive here, conveying every kind of goods from every people every hour, every day, so that the city is like a factory common to the whole earth. It is possible to see so many cargoes from India and even from Arabia Felix, if you wish, that one imagines that for the future the trees are left bare for the people there and that they must come here to beg for their own produce if they need anything. Again there can be seen clothing from Babylon and ornaments from the barbarian world beyond, which arrive in much larger quantity and more easily than if merchantmen bringing goods from Naxus or Cythnus had only to put into Athens. Your farmlands are Egypt, Sicily, and all of Africa which is cultivated. The arrivals and departures of the ships never stop, so that one would express admiration not only for the harbour, but even for the sea. Hesiod said about the limits of the Ocean, that it is a place where everything has been channelled into one beginning and end. So everything comes together here, trade, seafaring, farming, the scourings of the mines, all the crafts that exist or have existed, all that is produced and grown.

(trans. Behr)

### 113 *Expositio Totius Mundi* 23–33

In the late fourth century AD an anonymous author, who appears to have been active as a merchant, wrote a 'commercial geography' in which he describes the important ports of the Mediterranean, particularly those in the eastern part. He also lists the products for which each harbour is known, in particular agricultural produce and textiles. He does not forget to mention other characteristics of each town, as he goes along.

Then you have the whole area of Syria, which is divided in three provinces: Syria-Punica, Syria-Palestina and Coele-Syria. They have various distinguished and very large cities and I shall please my readers by giving an account of some of these.

The first is, of course, Antioch, a royal city, good in every respect where the lord of the world resides. It is a beautiful city, with outstanding public buildings. Receiving large numbers of people from all parts, it maintains all of them, (as) it abounds in all goods.

And then there are other cities, such as Tyre, which is highly prosperous as it is ardently engaged in all sorts of trade. There is perhaps no city in the East which is so densely populated, and it has also men whose fortunes stem from commerce and who are powerful in every respect.

And after that there is Berytus (Beirut), a truly delightful city, which has law schools and the entire Roman judicial system seems to depend from it. For there originate the learned men who all over the world advise the governors and who protect the provinces by their legal knowledge, and to them the ordinances of the law are sent.

Nearby you will find the city of Caesarea, which is likewise rather attractive, which abounds in everything, and which is distinguished over many cities for its layout. For they talk everywhere about its *tetrapylon*,[1] which is a unique and marvellous monument.

Then there are other cities, from which we must single out a few, because each one of them has something special. Therefore, there is also the good city of Laodicea, which imports and exports all kinds of trade, which is of great assistance to Antioch and the army.

Similarly, there is the very good city of Seleucia, which offers all the products that arrive there to Antiochia, which was mentioned above, not only fiscal goods but also privately shipped goods.

The Lord of the world, the Emperor Constans, recognizing its utility both for the city and the army, dug a channel through a very high mountain and let the sea in, and he constructed a large and fine harbour where the ships can come to safety, and where the fiscal cargoes will not perish.

Now we come to all the other cities. Ascalon and Gaza are distinguished cities, where commerce thrives, and which abound in all goods. They export with the bulk of their trade a very fine wine to Syria and to Egypt.

Neapolis is also a famous and truly notable city. Tripolis, Scythopolis and Byblos are also very industrious. Heliopolis, near Mount Lebanon, raises beautiful women, who are known everywhere as 'Lebanon's Ladies', and there they worship Venus in a splendid way: for it is said that she lives there and bestows the charm of beauty upon the women. And then there are also the cities of Sidon,

Sarepta, Ptolemais, Eleutheropolis, which are likewise very good, and so is Damascus.

Since we have described and spoken about the aforementioned cities only partially and since we have said that [. . . (lacuna). . . .]

The following cities produce linen: Scythopolis, Laodicea, Byblos, Tyre, Berytus and they export it all over the world, and they stand out by their wealth in every respect. Sarepta, Caesarea, and Neapolis, and to some extent also Lydda, export likewise real purple. And all the cities that I just mentioned are famous for their high production of grain, wine and oil, though they have all goods in abundance, hence they have the Nicolaus-date in the region of Palestine at a place called Jericho, and likewise the Damascus-date, and another variety which is smaller and pistachio nuts, and all sorts of fruits.

Since we have to describe their particular qualities, we must also say what attractions each city has to offer. Well, you have Antioch, which has many attractions, but the circus is the best. Why does it have all those things? Because the Emperor resides there, so, it is all necessary because of him. There are circuses also in Laodicea, Tyrus, Berytus and Caesarea, but Laodicea sends the best charioteers to the other cities. Tyrus and Berytus have mimes, Caesarea has pantomimes and Heliopolis has fluteplayers, mainly because the Muses from Mount Lebanon inspire them with a divine capacity to play. Finally, Gaza has also good declamators. It is said that it also has pancratiasts, that Ascalon has athletic wrestlers and that Castabala has acrobats.

All these cities are based on commerce and have men who are rich in everything, who distinguish themselves in oratory as well as through their actions and virtue. These cities have a moderate climate. This is only an incomplete description of Syria. For, we have left out many things, so that we would not appear to expand our essay too much, and so that we can also write about other cities.

*NOTE*

1 We do not know exactly what this building was.

## 114 C.P. Jones, *AJP* 99 (1989), 58

Ever since Syria became a Roman province in 64 BC, Syrian traders had travelled around the Roman world with their merchandise.

In Lyon, in the province of Gaul, there was a substantial Syrian community. The following text is the epitaph of a Syrian trader in Lyon. He claims that he came from a family who belonged to the élite of Laodicea. It is perhaps because of this background that he does his best to present his commercial activities as the bringing of gifts to the Gauls.

If you desire to know what mortal lies here, this writing will conceal nothing, but will tell all. Euteknios by surname, Julianus was his name, Laodicea his ancestral city, the admired ornament of Syria; honourable on his father's side,[1] and his mother had equal renown, good and upright, a man beloved by all, from whose tongue as he spoke to the Celts, persuasion flowed. Various the races that he visited, and many the peoples he came to know, and exercised the virtue of his soul among them. Constantly he gave himself over to waves and sea, bearing to the celts and the lands of the Occident all the gifts that god has bidden the all-bearing land of the Orient to bear; wherefore the threefold tribes of the Celts loved the man. He sailed [. . . .]

(trans. Jones)

*NOTE*

1 The word *entimos*, which is translated as honourable, indicates that members of his family had performed urban magistracies.

### 115 Dio Chrysostomus XXXV.14–16

For most cities in the Roman Empire that did not lie on the coast or along a major commercial route, trade did not often rise above a local or at best a regional level. This was the case in Celaena, a small city in the Phrygian highlands. Its situation is described clearly in a speech of Dio Chrysostomus (AD 40–*c.* 112) where he tries to make the best of Celaena's few strong points. He mentions that it serves its function as a market for the surrounding area, but it seems that Celaena managed to attract larger numbers of foreign traders only once every two years, when the Roman governor held court there.

[Y]ou stand as a bulwark in front of Phrygia and Lydia and Caria besides; and there are other tribes around you whose members are most numerous, Cappadocians and Pamphylians and Pisidians, and for them all your city constitutes a market and a place of meeting. And also many cities unknown to fame and many prosperous villages are subject to your sway. And a very great index of your power is found in the magnitude of the contributions with which you are assessed. For, in my opinion, just as those beasts of burden are judged to be most powerful which carry the greatest loads, so also it is reasonable to suppose that those cities are the most considerable which pay the largest assessments.

And what is more, the courts are in session every other year in Celaena, and they bring together an unnumbered throng of people – litigants, jurymen, orators, princes, attendants, slaves, pimps, muleteers, hucksters, harlots, and artisans. Consequently not only can those who sell goods obtain the highest prices, but also nothing in the city is out of work, neither the teams nor the houses nor the women. And this contributes not a little to prosperity; for wherever the greatest throng of people comes together, there necessarily we find money in greatest abundance, and it stands to reason that the place should thrive.

(trans. Cohoon)

In the second and third centuries AD merchants operating between Roman Britain and the German provinces often began their crossing of the North Sea at a place called Ganuentum, which now lies beneath the water of the Oosterschelde in the Dutch province of Zeeland. We know this because maritime archaeologists have brought to light the remains of a sanctuary and also a large number of votive inscriptions dedicated to a local goddess, Nehalennia, by grateful sailors and merchants after a safe journey.

The selection that follows is not only a striking illustration of the hazards of maritime trade, but also a valuable source of information on the movements of traders in this part of the Roman Empire, as they often gave an indication of their place of origin and of the sort of goods they were carrying. The spelling of the name of the goddess varies in the inscriptions, but the proper form seems to have been Nehalennia.

**116a *AE* (1973), 362**

To the goddess Nehalenia, Marcus Excingius Agricola, citizen of the Treveri (whose capital was Trier), salt merchant in the Colonia Claudia Arae Agrippinensium (Cologne), has fulfilled his vow, willingly and with reason.

**116b *AE* (1973), 364**

Sacred to the goddess Nehalenia, Caius Julius Florentius, citizen of Cologne, salt merchant, has fulfilled his vow, willingly and with reason, on his own behalf and that of his dependents.

**116c *AE* (1973), 365**

To Nehalennia. Lucius Secundius Similis and Titus Carinius Gratus, merchants in fish-sauce, have fulfilled their vow, willingly and with reason.

**116d *AE* (1983), 720**

To the goddess Nehalennia . . . Valerius Mar . . ., merchant trading in Cantia (Kent) and Gesoriacum (Boulogne) . . . for the protection of his merchandise.

**116e *AE* (1973), 370**

To the goddess Nehalennia, for the protection of his merchandise. Marcus Secundinius Silvanus, merchant in pottery trading in Britain, has fulfilled his vow, willingly and with reason.

**116f *AE* (1973), 372**

To the goddess Nehalennia, Vesigonius Martinus, citizen of the Secuani (who lived in the territory of Vesontio-Besançon), sailor, has fulfilled his vow, willingly and with reason.

**116g *AE* (1973), 375**

In honour of the Divine House (the Imperial house). To the goddess Nehalennia. Caius Catullinus Secco, merchant in fish-sauce, citizen of the Treveri, has fulfilled his vow willingly, on his own behalf and that of his dependents.

**116h *AE* (1975), 646**

To the goddess Nehalaenia. The altar in her honour which Hilarus *decurio* (town-councillor) of the Municipium of the Batavi (Nijmegen, on the lower Rhine) has vowed to her for the protection of his merchandise, he erected, willingly and with reason. In the year that Albinus and Maximus were consuls (AD 227).

**116i *AE* (1975), 647**

To the goddess Nehalaennia, for the protection of his merchandise. Caius Crescentius Florus has set up this monument, in obedience to her orders . . . .

**116j *AE* (1975), 651**

To the goddess Nehalennia. Placidus, son of Viducus, citizen of the Veliocasses (who lived in the territory of Rotomagus-Rouen), merchant trading in Britain, has fulfilled his vow, willingly and with reason.

**116k *AE* (1983), 721**

To the goddess Nehalennia. Publius Arisenius Marinus, freedman of Publius Arisenius V. . .hus, merchant trading in Britain, has fulfilled his vow, for the protection of his merchandise, willingly and with reason.

**116l *AE* (1980), 658**

To the goddess Nehalennia . . . Marcellus [*sevir augustalis* of the city] of the Raurici (=Augusta Raurica = Augst) [. . .] willingly and with reason.

# Part II

# The commodities

# 8 Grain

Hunger was never very far away in the ancient world. The Mediterranean climate, with its long dry summers, and its annual and regional variations in rainfall, made harvest failure a common feature of ancient life. Despite an ideology that stressed local self-sufficiency, no Greek *polis* could have survived for long without occasional imports of food (especially grain) from elsewhere. From an early period, therefore, transport of grain was not merely local (from the countryside to the town), but occurred on a regional or interregional scale. Of course, not all grain transport can be described as commercial exchange: the grain that was shipped was often tax grain or tribute grain; it could be presented as the gift of a ruler to a friendly nation, or it could be the produce of the estate of an absentee landowner, transported to the town where he lived. Yet grain was also one of the most important commercial cargoes of the ancient world.

## I GREEK CITIES AND THE IMPORT OF GRAIN

### 117 Herodotus VII.147

Athens was the largest Greek *polis* of the classical period; its population, including that of Attica, may have fluctuated between 120,000 and 250,000 in the fifth century, and between 120,000 and 200,000 in the fourth century BC. The Athenian population enjoyed a relatively high standard of living, and preferred bread as its staple food over *maza* (a porridge made of barley). Part of the wheat was produced in Attica itself, but from early on Athens had been a regular importer of foreign wheat, even if it became really dependent on imports only in the fifth century.

Early testimony to the regular grain imports to Athens is provided by an anecdote concerning the Persian king Xerxes, which Herodotus presents as an example of the royal *hybris*.

Xerxes had expressed a similar opinion on another occasion, when he was at Abydus and saw boats sailing down the Hellespont with cargoes of food from the Black Sea for Aegina and the Peloponnese. The nobles who were with him, learning that they were enemy vessels, were prepared to seize them, and kept their eye on the king in expectation of the order to do so. 'Where are they bound for?' Xerxes asked. 'To Persia's enemies, my lord,' came the answer, 'with a cargo of grain.' 'Well,' said the king, 'are we not bound ourselves for the same destination? And does not our equipment include grain amongst other things? I do not see that the men in those ships are doing us any harm in carrying our grain for us.'

(trans. De Sélincourt)

### 118 Demosthenes, *Against Leptines* 31–3

More than a century later, Athens' dependence on foreign grain had not diminished. In the following speech against a certain Leptines, Demosthenes presents some calculations of the amounts of grain that were imported to Athens from the Black Sea area, in order to emphasize the important role of Leucon, the ruler of the Bosporan kingdom on the Crimea (389–349 BC).

For you are aware that we consume more imported corn than any other nation. Now the corn that comes to our ports from the Black Sea is equal to the whole amount from all other places of export. And this is not surprising; for not only is that district most productive of corn, but also Leucon, who controls the trade, has granted exemption from dues to merchants conveying corn to Athens, and he proclaims that those bound for your port shall have priority of lading. For Leucon, enjoying exemption for himself and his children, has granted exemption to every one of you. See what this amounts to. He exacts a toll of one-thirtieth from exporters of corn from his country. Now from the Bosporus there come to Athens about four hundred thousand bushels; the figures can be checked by the books of the grain-commissioners. So for each three hundred thousand bushels he makes us a present of ten thousand bushels, and for the remaining hundred thousand a present of roughly three thousand. Now, so little danger is there of his depriving our state of this gift, that he has opened another depot at Theudosia, which our merchants say is not at all inferior to the Bosporus, and there, too, he has granted us the same exemption. I omit much that might be said about the other benefits conferred upon you by this prince and also by his ancestors, but the year before last, when there was a universal shortage of grain, he not only sent enough for your needs, but such a quantity in addition that Callisthenes had a surplus of fifteen talents of silver to dispose of.

(trans. Vince)

### 119 Demosthenes, *Against Lacritus* 51

The import of sufficient amounts of grain was major concern of the Athenian state. Each month the Athenian assembly discussed the current state of the city's grain supply. Demosthenes, in his speech against Lacritus (see text no. 68), even quotes a law forbidding any Athenian to transport grain to any other harbour than Athens.

It shall be unlawful for any Athenian or any alien residing at Athens or for any person over whom they have control, to lend money on any vessel which is not going to bring to Athens grain or the other articles specifically mentioned. And if any man lends out money contrary to this decree, information and an account of the money shall be laid before the harbour-masters in the same manner as is provided in regard to the ship and the grain. And he shall have no right to bring action for the money which he has lent for a voyage to any other place than to Athens, and no magistrate shall bring any such suit to trial.

(trans. Vince)

### 120 Lysias, *Against the Grain Dealers* 11–17

Lysias' speech against the grain dealers was probably delivered in 386 BC. A group of retailers had formed a cartel in order to keep down the wholesale price. They had been stockpiling grain, and were now selling it for a high price to the population. Although the speculation in itself was not illegal, there was a law which forbade retailers to buy more than fifty baskets of grain at a time; the retailers were now charged under this law.

But in fact, gentlemen of the jury, I believe . . . they will repeat, perhaps, what they said before the council – that it was in kindness to the city that they bought up the grain, so that they might sell it to you at as reasonable a price as possible. But I will give you a very strong and signal proof that they are lying. If they were doing this for your benefit, they ought to have been found selling it at the same price for a number of days, until the stock that they had bought up was exhausted. But in fact they were selling at a profit of a drachma several times in the same day, as though they were buying by the medimnus at a time. I adduce you as witnesses of this. And it seems to me a strange thing that, when they have to contribute to a special levy of which everyone is to have knowledge, they refuse, making poverty their pretext; but illegal acts, for which death is the penalty, and in which secrecy was important to them, these they assert that they committed in kindness to you. Yet you are all aware that they are the last persons to whom such statements are appropriate. For their interests are the opposite of other men's: they make most profit when, on some bad news reaching the city, they sell their grain at a high price. And they are so delighted to see your disasters that they either get news of them in advance of anyone else, or fabricate the rumour themselves; now it is the loss of your ships in the Black Sea, now the capture of vessels on their outward voyage by the Lacedaemonians, now the blockade of your trading ports, or the impending rupture of the truce; and they have carried their enmity to such lengths that they choose the same critical moments as your foes to overreach you. For, just when you find yourselves worst off for grain, these persons snap it up and refuse to sell it, in order to prevent our disputing about the price: we are to be glad enough if we come away from them with a purchase made at any price, however high. And thus at times, although there is peace, we are besieged by these men. So long is it now that the city has been convinced of their knavery and disaffection that, while for the sale of all other commodities you have appointed the market-clerks as controllers, for this trade alone you elect special grain-controllers by lot; and often you have been known to inflict the extreme penalty on those officials, who were citizens, for having failed to defeat the villainy of these men. Now, what should be your treatment of the actual offenders, when you put to death even those who are unable to control them?

(adapted from Lamb)

## 121 *SIG*³ 354

When grain was in short supply (and that happened all too often), prices soared, to the benefit of landowners and merchants. Urban authorities had only limited means of reducing the effects of a food crisis, and they often had to rely on the willingness of foreign merchants to supply grain. When a merchant was prepared not to charge the full market price, he could expect a reward in the form of an honorary inscription set up by the city. An inscription of *c.* 300 BC, found in the theatre of Ephesus, praises a Rhodian merchant for selling grain at a low price. He was duly rewarded with a grant of citizenship.

Resolved by the council and the people; Dion son of Diopithes moved: since Agathocles son of Hegemon of Rhodes, when he was importing grain to the city amounting to 14,000 *hekteis* and found that the grain in the agora was being sold at more than 6 drachmas, he was persuaded by the *agoranomos*[1] and wished to do a favour to the people, and sold all his grain more cheaply than it was being sold in the agora, be it resolved by the people, to grant citizenship to Agathocles of Rhodes on a basis of full equality, to himself and his descendants; the priests shall allot him a tribe and *chiliastys*[2] and the temple administrators shall inscribe these honours in the sanctuary of Artemis, where the other grants of citizenship are inscribed, so that all may know that the people knows how to return thanks to its benefactors. He was allotted the tribe Bembine and the *chiliastys* Aegoteus.

(trans. Austin)

*NOTES*

1 In Greek cities, a magistrate in charge of supervision of the agora.
2 Subdivision of a tribe.

### 122 Tod II.30

The importance of foreign grain to a small city such as Teos, on the west coast of Asia Minor, is borne out by a law of 475–470 BC, which deals with grain imports. People who prevented the import of grain or re-exported grain could expect the death penalty.

Whoever makes drugs that are poisonous (for use) against the Teians as a community or against a private citizen, that man shall die, both himself and his family. If into the land of Teos anyone prevents grain from being imported by any pretext or device, either by sea or by the mainland, or, after it is imported, re-export it, that man shall die, both himself and his family.

(trans. Fornara)

### 123 Tod II.196

The major grain-exporting areas of antiquity were Egypt and the Black Sea area, but northern Africa was also an important exporter of grain. In an inscription which dates from between 331 and 324 BC the city of Cyrene lists the areas and cities to which it has 'given' grain during a period of food crises.

Sosias, son of Calliades was priest. The city gave grain to all these cities mentioned below, when the grain-shortage occurred in Greece. To the Athenians 100,000; to Olympias 60,000; to the Argives 50,000; to the Larisans 50,000; to the Corinthians 50,000; to Cleopatra 50,000;

to the Rhodians 30,000; to the Sicyonians 30,000; to the Meliboeans 20,000; to the Megarians 20,000; to the T[enian]s 20,000; to the Les[bian]s 15,000; to the Therans 15,000; to the Oeteans 15,000; to the Ambraciots 15,000; to the Leucadians 15,000; to the Carystians 15,000; to Olympias 12,600; to the Atragians of Thessaly 10,000; to the Kythnians 10,000; to the Opuntians 10,000; to the Cydonians 10,000; to the Coans 10,000; to the Parians 10,000; to the Delphians 10,000; to the Cnosians 10,000; to the Boeotians of Tanagra 10,000; to the Gortynians 10,000; to the Eleans 10,000; to the Palaereans of Acarnania 10,000; to the Megarians 10,000; to the Meliboeans 8,500; to the Phliasians 8,000; to the Hermionians 8,000; to the Oetaeans 6,400; to the Troezenians 6,000; to the Plataeans 6,000; to the Iulietans on Ceos 5,000; to the Aeginetans 5,000; to the Astypalaeans 5,000; to the Cytherans 5,000; to the Hyrtacinians 5,000; to the Aeginetans 5,000; to the Carthaeans on Ceos 4,000; to the Cytherans 3,100; to the Ceans 3,000; to the Ilyrians 3,000; to the Coresians on Ceos 3,000; to the Ambraciots 1,500; to the Icetyrians 1,000; to the [C]nosians 900.

## II GRAIN FOR ROME

Rome had perhaps one million inhabitants in the early Principate. Its demand for grain was huge, and could not be met from Italian sources alone. Sicily had long been an important source of grain, but from the second century BC onwards increasing amounts of grain were imported from northern Africa and Egypt.

### 124 *Epitome de Caesaribus* I.6

It is difficult to calculate the exact amount of grain imported by Rome. A very high figure, 400,000 tonnes, is reached by combining two literary texts: a fragment from the fourth-century *Epitome de Caesaribus*, and a passage from Flavius Josephus' *Jewish War*. Modern estimates are that the city of Rome consumed around 30 million *modii*, or 200,000 tonnes of wheat per year.

In his (sc. Augustus') days twenty million *modii* of grain were imported each year from Egypt to the city.

### 125 Flavius Josephus, *Jewish War* II.382–3 and 385–6

To these 20 million *modii* (about 130,000 tonnes) of Egyptian grain we should add another 40 million *modii*, if we can believe Flavius Josephus, who reports that Africa supplied twice as much grain to Rome as did Egypt.

This third of the whole world, the mere enumeration of whose nations is no easy task, bounded by the Atlantic and the Pillars of Hercules, and supporting right up to the Red Sea the thousands of Ethiopians, is subdued in its entirety; and these peoples, besides their annual crops, which feed for eight months of the year the populace of Rome, pay tribute of every kind and for the needs of the Empire willingly submit to taxation. . . . This country, which stretches as far as Ethiopia and Arabia Felix, which is the port for India, which has a population of seven and a half million, excluding the inhabitants of Alexandria, as may be estimated from the poll-tax returns, this country, I say, does not disdain to submit to Roman domination; and yet what a stimulus to revolt she has in Alexandria, so populous, so wealthy, so vast! The length of that city is thirty furlongs, its breadth not less than ten; the tribute which she pays to Rome in one month surpasses that which you pay in a year; besides money she sends grain to feed Rome for four months.

**126 Pliny, *Natural History* XVIII.66–8**

Rome was not supplied by these provinces alone. Pliny the Elder mentions some other grain-exporting areas:

At the present the lightest in weight among the kinds of wheat imported to Rome is the wheat of Gaul, and that brought from the Chersonese, as they do not exceed twenty pounds a peck, if one weighs the grain by itself. Sardinian grain adds half a pound to this figure, and Alexandrian a third of a pound more – this is also the weight of Sicilian wheat – while that of Southern Spain scores a whole pound more and that of Africa a pound and three-quarters. In Italy north of the Po the peck of emmer to my knowledge weighs twenty-five pounds, and in the Chiusi neighbourhood even twenty-six pounds. It is a fixed law of nature that in any kind of commissariat bread a third part is added in the making to the weight of the grain, just as that the best wheat is that which absorbs three quarts of water into the peck of grain kneaded. Some kinds of grain used by themselves give their full weight, for instance a peck of Balearic wheat produces thirty-five pounds of bread, but some only do so when blended – for example, Cyprian wheat and Alexandrian, which used by themselves do not go beyond twenty pounds a peck. Cyprus wheat is of a dusky colour and makes black bread, and consequently the white Alexandrian is mixed with it, and that gives twenty-five pounds of bread to the peck. The wheat of the Thebaid in Egypt makes a pound more.

(trans. Rackman)

### 127 Cicero, *On the Appointment of Gnaeus Pompeius* 44

Not all the food crises of antiquity could be attributed to natural causes; man made crises were at least as common, and perhaps even more severe. During the late Republic Rome was repeatedly confronted with more or less serious subsistence crises. In 67 BC Roman grain convoys were intercepted by pirates, who operated even in the waters of Italy. This called for emergency measures and Pompey received extraordinary powers. This proved an instant success: on the very day that Pompey was appointed, the prices plummeted, which suggests that speculation and stockpiling rather than the actions of the pirates were the main causes of the grain shortage.

Do you really think that anywhere in the whole wide world is so desolate that it has not heard the story of that great day when the whole population of Rome, thronging into the Forum and filling every temple that commands a view of this platform, demanded the appointment of Gnaeus Pompey alone to be their general in a war that threatened the safety of the world? And so, without going on to prove by the examples of other men how great is the influence of prestige in war, let me quote Pompey once again as an example of every form of distinction: on the day on which you appointed him commander-in-chief of the naval operations against the pirates, his name alone and the hopes which it inspired caused a sudden fall in the price of wheat, after a time of extreme dearth and scarcity in the grain supply, to as low a level as could possibly have been reached after a bumper harvest in stable peaceful conditions.

### 128 Cicero, *On his House* 11

Speculation was more obviously the reason for the high grain prices some years later, in 58–56 BC. Cicero explains the food shortage thus:

The reason for the famine was partly that the grain-growing provinces had no grain; partly that it had been exported to other countries, the demands of the dealers being, as we are asked to believe, extortionate; partly that it was being kept stored in custody, in order that its alleviating effect in the actual throes of famine might be more gratifying; it was to be produced as an unlooked-for surprise.

(trans. Watts – adapted)

In the Principate more lasting solutions were found to Rome's grain-supply problems. Augustus had on several occasions to intervene personally to alleviate grain shortages, but he also made structural improvements to the system of supply. His annexation of Egypt ensured its role as a major supplier to Rome. Another important step was the creation of the office of prefect of the grain supply. Yet these measures did not prove sufficient and later emperors had to take further action.

## 129 Suetonius, *Claudius* 18–19

The Roman authorities left the shipment of grain to private shipowners and entrepreneurs, for whom this was profitable enough. From time to time, however, emperors took measures to make it more attractive to invest in grain transport. In AD 51 the emperor Claudius was forced to take such measures.

Claudius always interested himself in the proper upkeep of city buildings and the regular arrival of corn supplies. When an obstinate fire ravaged the Aemilian quarter, he lodged at the Election hut on the Campus Martius for two nights running; and, because a force of Guards and another of Palace servants proved insufficient to cope with the blaze, made the magistrates summon the commons from every City district and then sat, with bags of coin piled before him, recruiting fire-fighters; whom he paid, on the nail, whatever seemed a suitable fee for their services.

Once, after a series of droughts had caused a scarcity of grain, a mob stopped Claudius in the Forum and pelted him so hard with curses and stale crusts that he had difficulty in regaining the Palace by a side-door; as a result he took all possible steps to import corn, even during the winter months – insuring merchants against the loss of their ships in stormy weather (which guaranteed them a good return on their ventures), and offering a bounty for every new grain-transport built, proportionate to its tonnage.

The shipowner, if he happened to be a Roman citizen, was exempted from the Papian-Poppaean Law which made marriage obligatory; if only a Latin, acquired full Roman citizenship; if a woman, enjoyed the privileges granted to mothers of four children. These regulations have never since been modified.

(trans. Graves)

## 130 M. Wörrle, *Chiron* 1 (1971), 325

The grain supply of Rome remained vulnerable to disturbances, and the arrival of the grain fleet from Alexandria was a major event (see text no. 211). The annexation of Egypt by Augustus may have presented some difficulties to the grain supply of cities in the eastern part of the Mediterranean, which used to rely on Egyptian grain. An inscription from Ephesus (second century AD) lays down the principle: the needs of the city of Rome are served first. The

Ephesians are granted the right to head the queue of other cities waiting for Egyptian grain.

(Considering) the greatness of your eminent city, and the number of people who live with you. . . . It is clear that you will make prudent use of this agreement, bearing in mind that first the imperial city should have a bounteous supply of wheat procured and assembled for its market, and then the other cities may also receive provisions in plenty. If, as we pray, the Nile provides us with a flood at the customary level, and a bountiful harvest of wheat is produced among the Egyptians, then you will be among the first after the homeland.

# 9 Wool and textiles

In the economies of pre-industrial Europe, the production of and trade in textiles was the most prominent economic sector after agriculture. The greater part of the textile trade involved cheap and medium-priced textiles, which were produced for local or regional markets. The demand from the élite was for the more expensive, high-quality cloth, which a small number of specialized textile towns produced for an international market.

We are less well informed about the textile trade in antiquity. It is likely, however, that, in the Roman Empire in particular, textiles were an important trade item. Even the poorer classes normally bought their clothing, which was often produced locally. Their aggregate demand should not be underestimated. Elite demand was for more expensive clothing, in which there was a very profitable long-distance trade.

### 131 Pliny, *Natural History* VIII.190–3

The trade in raw materials, unprocessed or semi-processed wool, was not less important than the trade in textiles. The Elder Pliny lists, in his *Naturalis Historia* (Natural History), several varieties of high-quality wool.

The most highly esteemed wool is the Apulian and the kind that is called in Italy wool of the Greek breed and elsewhere Italian wool. The third place is held by the sheep of Miletus. The Apulian fleeces are short in the hair, and not of great repute except for cloaks; they have a very high reputation in the districts of Tarentum and Canossa, as have the Laodicean fleeces of the same breed in Asia. No white fleece is valued above that from the district of the Po, and none has hitherto gone beyond the price of 100 sesterces a pound. Sheep are not shorn everywhere – in some places the practice survives of plucking off the wool. There are several sorts of colour, in fact even names are lacking for the wools which are variously designated after their places of origin: Spain has the principal black wool fleeces, Pollentia near the Alps white, Asia the red fleeces that they call Erythrean, Baetica the same, Canossa tawny, Tarentum also a dark colour of its own. All fresh fleeces have a medicinal property. Istrian and Liburnian fleece is nearer to hair than wool, and not suitable for garments with a soft nap; and the same applies to the fleece that Salacia in Lusitania advertises by its check pattern. There is a similar wool in the district of the Fishponds in the province of Narbonne, and also in Egypt, which is used for darning clothes worn by use and making them last again for a long period. Also the coarse hair of a shaggy fleece has a very ancient popularity in carpets: Homer is evidence that they were undoubtedly in use even in very early times. Different methods of dyeing these fleeces are practised by the Gauls and by the Parthian races. Self-felted fleeces make clothing, and also if vinegar is added withstand even steel, nay more even fire, the latest method of cleaning them. In fact fleeces drawn from the coppers of the polishers serve as stuffing for cushions, I believe by a Gallic invention: at all events at the present day it is classified under Gallic names. And I could not easily say at what period this began; for people in old times had bedding of straw, in the same way as in camp now. Frieze cloaks began within my father's memory and cloaks with hair on both sides within my own, as also shaggy body-belts; moreover weaving a broad-striped tunic after the manner of a frieze cloak is coming in for the first time now. Black fleeces will not take dye of any colour; we will discuss the dyeing of the other sorts in their proper places under the head of marine shellfish or the nature of various plants.

(trans. Rackman – adapted)

### 132 *IGSK* I 15

Pliny mentions a variety of wool which he calls 'Erythraean', and which appears to have been a collective name for different varieties of a reddish wool from Asia Minor. This wool was named after the city of Erythrae, where it was marketed. A fourth-century (BC) inscription, which was found in Chios, but which has been ascribed to Erythrae, contains several market regulations concerning the trade in wool.

. . . and each dealer is to weigh out the amount of wool that he is selling; he is to weigh honestly, and anyone who cheats is liable to pay twenty drachmas for each [occasion]; the *agoranomos* is to exact payment. Sales may take place up to noon. When it rains no one is to put wool on display. No one is to sell the wool of one-year old sheep. Anyone who does so is to be fined two drachmas a day by the *agoranomos*. No [merchant] and no huckster is to sell either wool or flocks of wool [from the fleece?] to anyone from anywhere else than from [the balance? If he does so,] the wool is confiscated and he is to pay twenty drachmas. And all the wool sold otherwise than from the balance will be auctioned publicly by the *prytanees*.

### 133 *Price Edict* XXV[1]

In AD 301 the emperor Diocletian issued a Price Edict, in order to fix maximum prices and wages. The Edict does not seem to have been very successful, but it is still of interest to us, as it lists several categories of products which were the object of interregional trade during that period. In chapter 25, some prices are listed for different varieties of wool (see text no. 140).

Concerning wool

| | |
|---|---|
| Wool, from Mutina, with a golden sheen, washed, | 1 pound, denarii 300 |
| Wool, from Mutina, darker, | 1 pound, denarii 200 |
| Marine wool, | 1 pound, denarii 400 |
| Wool, from Altinum, | 1 pound, denarii 200 |
| Wool, from Tarentum, washed, | 1 pound, denarii 175 |
| Wool, from Laodicea, washed, | 1 pound, denarii 150 |
| Wool, from Asturia, washed, | 1 pound, denarii 100 |
| Wool, of the best middle quality, washed, | 1 pound, denarii 50 |
| All other wool, washed, | 1 pound, denarii 25 |
| Hare's wool, from the back, | 1 pound, denarii [. . .] |
| Hare's wool, mixed, | 1 pound, denarii 100 |
| Wool, from Aria (?), | 1 pound, denarii 150 |
| Wool, from the Atrebates, | 1 pound, denarii 200 |

*NOTE*

1 Based on S. Lauffer, *Diokletians Preisedikt* (Berlin 1971), and the fragment published by J. Reynolds, 'Diocletian's Edict on maximum prices: the chapter on wool', *ZPE* 42 (1981), 283–4.

Although textile production for local use took place in all parts of the Empire, there were some cities which seem to have specialized in production of clothing for export markets. Ancient textile trade, in contrast to medieval practice, was in woven garments, not in bales of cloth.

### 134 Strabo V.1.12

One of the cities renowned for their textile production was Patavium, modern Padua. Strabo mentions that the area around that city produced a good quality of wool, which was used for expensive clothes.

As for wool, the soft kind is produced by the regions round Mutina and the River Scultenna (the finest wool of all); the coarse, by Liguria and the country of the Symbri, from which the greater part of the households of the Italiotes are clothed; and the medium, by the regions round Patavium, from which are made the expensive carpets and covers and everything of this kind that is woolly either on both sides or only on one.

(trans. Jones)

### 135 Strabo V.1.7

The main market for the textiles of Patavium was the city of Rome. In another passage Strabo discusses the wealth of Patavium and implies that it was based on the export of clothes to Rome.

These cities, then, are situated considerably above the marshes; and near them is Patavium, the best of all the cities in that part of the country, since this city by recent census, so it is said, had five hundred knights, and, besides, in ancient times used to send forth an army of one hundred and twenty thousand. And the quantities of manufactured goods which Patavium sends to Rome to market – clothing of all sorts and many other things – show what a goodly store of men it has and how skilled they are in the arts.

(trans. Jones)

### 136 *CIL* V 5929

In Mediolanum (modern Milan), which also lies in the Po Valley, we find the epitaph of a certain M. Matutinius Maximus. He was a citizen of the Mediomatrici (who lived in the territory of Metz), and he was probably involved in the trade in *sagi* (woollen cloaks) between the two cities.

To the Departed Spirits and the Everlasting Freedom from Care. For Marcus Matutinius Maximus, *negotiator sagaricus*, (cloak merchant), citizen of the Mediomatrici. M. Matutinius Marcus, his brother, and C. Sanctinius Sanc[tus] had the tomb erected.

The region around the neighbouring cities of Hierapolis and Laodicea in Phrygia possessed several features which favoured a flourishing textile trade. The wool produced in this area was of high quality, and the water from the mineral sources in Hierapolis was particularly suited to the washing and dyeing of wool.

## 137 W. Judeich, *Altertümer von Hierapolis*, Jahrbuch des kaiserlich deutschen archäologischen Instituts, Ergänzungsheft 4 (Berlin 1898), 156

Washing and dyeing were important economic activities in Hierapolis. This is suggested by the various associations of wool-washers, dyers and purple-dealers which we know from the epigraphic record. One purple-dealer from Hierapolis was accepted as a member of the local council, which implies both considerable wealth and social respectability.

This is the tomb of Marcus Aurelius Alexander Moschianus; councillor and purple-dealer.

## 138 *Expositio Totius Mundi* 42

Laodicea was similarly famous for its high-quality wool, but we also have evidence for cloth production taking place in Laodicea. The author of the *Expositio Totius Mundi* (see no. 113) states that Laodicea was famous for the production of a special garment, the *Laodicena*.

There is also Phrygia, which is a good region, and which has produced many men of valour, according to the writings of the ancients, like Homer and Vergil, and others who wrote about the wars of these Phrygians with the Greeks. It is said that it also has a very large city, Laodicea, which exports a garment of one piece, which is named after it, and which is called *Laodicena*.

## 139 *CIL* XIII 2003[1]

An inscription from Lyon may contain a further reference to the Laodicean textile trade. It is the epitaph for a certain Julius Verecundus, who was a *negotiator Laodicenarius*; this could mean that he was a textile merchant who specialized in the *Laodicena* or in other textiles from Laodicea.

To the Departed Spirits and the eternal memory of Julius Verecundus, *negotiator Laodicenarius* (merchant in cloth goods of Laodicea) and of Julius Verissimus and Julius Verecundus, his sons. Aurelia Aquinia has seen to the erection of this monument, for her dead husband and sons, with whom she lived for twenty-two years and five months, without the slightest pain to the heart; and she has dedicated it under the sign of the *ascia* (the mason's trowel).

### *NOTE*

1 Text based on J. Rougé, '*CIL* XIII, 2003. Un negotiator Laudecenarius à Lyon', *ZPE* 27 (1977), 263–9.

## 140 *Price Edict* XIX[1]

The Price Edict does not only list wool and other raw materials. In the chapter that is titled 'On clothing', it also sets the prices for various garments. The geographical indications after each garment may refer to the places of production, but it is also possible that they refer to the varieties of wool which were used.

| Concerning clothing | |
|---|---|
| Hooded cloak, Laodicean | denarii 4,500 |
| Hooded cloak, Laodicean, resembling one from the Nervii, | denarii 10,000 |
| Dalmatic, unmarked, Laodicean, twilled, | denarii 2,000 |
| Bordered tunic, Laodicean, to be sold at a price in which the value of the purple has been included. | |
| Dalmatic, of hare's wool [. . .], man's having one pound of vegetable purple, | denarii [. . .] |
| Tunic, [of hare's wool having one pound of] purple, | denarii [. . .] |
| Dalmatic, with hood, hare's wool having one pound of vegetable purple, | denarii [. . .] |
| Hooded cloak, Nervian, or in the colour of a lion's skin first quality, | denarii 15,000 |
| Hooded cloak, Taurogastric(?), | denarii 12,000 |
| Hooded cloak, Ripesian, | denarii 8,000 |
| Hooded cloak, Britannic, | denarii 6,000 |
| Hooded cloak, Melitomagensian (?), | denarii 6,000 |
| Hooded cloak, Canusian, striped, first quality, | denarii 4,000 |
| Hooded cloak, Numidian, | denarii 3,000 |
| Hooded cloak, Argolic, first quality, | denarii 6,000 |
| Hooded cloak, Achaean or Phrygian, best quality, | denarii 2,000 |
| Hooded cloak, African, | denarii 1,500 |
| *Banata*(?) Noric, doubled or *katabion*(?), | denarii 20,000 |
| *Fedox* (goat's?), Noric, best quality, | denarii 10,000 |
| *Banata*(?), Gallic, | denarii 15,000 |
| *Fedox*(?), Gallic, | denarii 8,000 |
| Shirt, Noric, | denarii 1,500 |
| Shirt, Gallic, | denarii 1,250 |
| Shirt, Numidian, | denarii 600 |
| Shirt, Phrygian or Bessian, | denarii 600 |
| Hooded cape, Laodicean, best quality, | denarii 5,000 |
| Hooded cape, Balusian, | denarii 4,000 |
| Cloak with clasp, Raetian, | denarii 12,500 |
| Cloak with clasp, Treveran, | denarii 8,000 |

| | |
|---|---|
| Cloak with clasp, Potoevian, | denarii 5,000 |
| Cloak with clasp, African, | denarii 2,000 |
| Mantle, Dardanian, doubled, best quality, | denarii 12,500 |
| Mantle, Dardanian, single, best quality, | denarii 7,000 |
| Short cloak, | denarii 1,000 |
| Cloak, African, | denarii 500 |
| Cloak, Gallic, that is from the Ambiani or the Bituriges, | denarii 8,000 |
| Shirt of hare's wool from the back, with purple stripes [having] six *unciae* of purple, | denarii 6,000 |
| Dalmatic, male, of hare's wool, with purple stripes, [having six] *unciae* of purple, | denarii 7,000 |
| Dalmatic, hooded, of hare's wool, with purple stripes, [having] one half pound [of purple], | denarii 7,000 |

*NOTE*

1 Text based on S. Lauffer, *Diokletians Preisedikt* (Berlin 1971), and J.M. Reynolds, XIII, in: C. Roueché, *Aphrodisias in Late Antiquity* (London 1989).

# 10 Wine and oil

The contribution of archaeology to the study of ancient trade has been considerable. This holds true in particular for the trade in such cash crops as wine and oil, and also *garum* (fish sauce)[1] since the containers in which they were transported, amphorae, have survived in large numbers.

The archaeological data supplement the literary and epigraphic evidence, and have given rise to a picture of a lively interregional trade in wine and oil.

*NOTE*

1 See nos 116c and 116g.

The transport of wine occurred predominantly between the vineyard and the neighbouring town. More exclusive wines, the *grands crus* of antiquity, were shipped over longer distances to élite customers. The reputations of some wine-producing regions of Syria, Etruria and northern Africa lasted throughout antiquity. The Greek islands of Rhodes and Cos also produced high-quality wines. From the third century BC Latium and Campania in Italy intensified their production of exclusive wines, which were exported in large quantities.

The amphorae which have been found in the shipwrecks of this period off the coasts of Italy, southern France and Spain were predominantly Italian. Shipwrecks of the Imperial period show, however, a predominance of amphorae from southern Gaul and Rhodes.

### 141 Homer, *Iliad* VII.465–75

In the seventh book of the Iliad, Homer describes how the Achaeans laboured on a defensive wall around their ships and encampment. After their work was done, they feasted all night and drank wine imported from Lesbos.

And the sun set, and the Achaeans' work was done. Then they slaughtered oxen in their huts and took their supper. And ships had come from Lemnos bringing wine, many of them, sent there by Iason's son Euneus, borne by Hypsipyle to Iason, shepherd of the people. The son of Iason had given a special cargo of wine, a thousand measures, for the sons of Atreus, Agamemnon and Menelaus. From these ships the long-haired Achaeans bought their wine. Some paid in bronze, some in gleaming iron, some in hides, some in live oxen, some in slaves: and they made a generous feast. Then all night long there was feasting for the long-haired Achaeans, and for the Trojans and their allies throughout the city.

(trans. Hammond)

### 142 Herodotus III.6

Modern distribution maps of the finds of amphorae are sometimes used to reconstruct ancient trade routes. That the presence or absence of amphorae cannot always be used as an unproblematic indicator of the trade in wine or oil is demonstrated by the following passage from Herodotus.

I will now mention something of which few voyagers to Egypt are aware. Throughout the year, not only from all parts of Greece but from Phoenicia as well, wine is imported into Egypt in earthenware jars; yet one might say that not a single empty wine-jar is to be seen anywhere in the country. The obvious question is: what becomes of them? I will explain. The mayor of each place has orders to collect all the jars from his town and send them to Memphis, and the people of Memphis have to fill them with water and send them to this tract of desert in Syria. In this way every fresh jar of wine imported into Egypt, and there emptied of its content, finds its way into Syria to join the previous ones.

(trans. De Sélincourt)

### 143 H.W. Pleket, *Epigraphica* I, no. 2, I and II

In the late fifth century BC, the authorities of the island of Thasos in the northern Aegean issued a decree concerning the trade in wine on Thasos and its mainland territories.

I

Neither sweet wine nor (ordinary) wine from the crop on the vines shall be bought before the first of Plynterion.[1] Whoever [transgresses] and buys it shall have to pay a fine of stater for stater, [half] to the city, half to the one who has prosecuted (him). The form of suit shall be the same as in cases of violence. But if someone buys wine in wine jars, the purchase shall be valid if (the seller) has stamped a seal on the jars. (vacat.)

II

[. . . the] penalties and deposits shall be the same. If no one makes the deposit, the Commissioners for the Mainland are to bring suit. Whenever they win the suit, the whole of the penalty shall belong to the city. If the Commissioners do not bring suit, though they have the information, they themselves shall have to pay a penalty of double (the amount). Whoever wishes may bring suit (against them) in the same way, and he shall keep half of the penalty, and the suit shall be granted by the *demiourgoi*[2] against the Commissioners in the same way. No boat of Thasos shall import foreign wine within (the points of) Athos and Pacheia. If it does, (the owner) shall have to pay the same penalty. The trial and the deposits shall be the same. Neither out of amphorae nor out of a cask nor out of a 'false-jar' shall anyone sell by the *kotyle*[3] (rather than wholesale). Whenever someone does sell (by the *kotyle*), the form of suit and deposits and penalties are to be the same as for adulterating (wine) with water. (vacat.)

(trans. Fornara)

*NOTES*

1 The island Thasos had its own calendar; we do not know which month Plynterion was.

2 Magistrates of high rank. Virtually no detailed information about them exists.

3 A liquid measure of nearly half a pint.

## 144 Diodorus Siculus V.26.2–3

When ancient authors discuss foreign nations and peoples, they invariably draw attention to their attitudes to wine. The degree to which patterns of production and consumption conformed to Mediterranean standards was seen as an index of civilization.

In the days of Diodorus Siculus (first century BC), the inhabitants of southern Gaul had learned to appreciate wine, but were not yet able to produce their own. This offered great opportunities to Italian merchants.

Furthermore, since temperateness of climate is destroyed by the excessive cold, the land produces neither wine nor oil, and as a consequence those Gauls who are deprived of these fruits make a drink out of barley which they call zythos or beer, and they also drink the water with which they cleanse their honeycombs. The Gauls are exceedingly addicted to the use of wine and fill themselves with the wine which is brought into their country by merchants, drinking it unmixed, and since they partake of this drink without moderation by reason of their craving for it, when they are drunken they fall into a stupor or a state of madness. Consequently many of the Italian traders, induced by the love of money which characterizes them, believe that the love of wine of these Gauls is their own godsend. For these transport the wine on the navigable rivers by means of boats and through the level plain on wagons, and receive for it an incredible price; for in exchange for a jar of wine they receive a slave, getting a servant in return for the drink.

(trans. Oldfather)

Olive oil was an essential product in all periods of antiquity. It was used for the preparation of meals, and as fuel for oil lamps, as well as for personal hygiene. Oil was produced in all parts of the Mediterranean, but some areas were particularly renowned for their oil. Finds of amphorae show that the islands of Rhodes, Cnidos and Chios played an important role in the oil trade of the Greek world. Oil from Attica, and from some of the islands, enjoyed a high reputation, and was even exported to the western Mediterranean.

### 145 Plutarch, *Solon* XXIV.1

Attica was renowned for its oil production and in normal years the production exceeded local demand. We are already hearing of Athenian oil exports in the sixth century BC, when, probably in the context of a food crisis, Solon forbade the export from Athens of any product other than oil.

Oil was the only product of Attica which Solon allowed to be exported, and he decreed that any offender against this regulation should be solemnly cursed by the archon, or else should pay 100 drachmas to the public treasury. This law is inscribed upon the first of his tables, so that there seems to be some evidence for the tradition that the export of figs was prohibited in ancient times, and that those who exposed or informed against such exporters were called sycophants, or 'fig-declarers'.

(trans. Scott-Kilvert)

### 146 Aristotle, *Economics* II.2.16

Oil exports were sometimes used to alleviate the consequences of a food shortage. In the fourth century BC, the authorities of Clazomenae, on the west coast of Asia Minor, used local surpluses of oil to finance a grain fund.

The people of Clazomenae, suffering from shortage of grain and scarcity of funds, passed a resolution that any private citizens who had stores of oil should lend it to the state at interest, this being a produce which their land bears in abundance. The loan arranged, they hired vessels and sent them to the depots whence they obtained their grain, and bought a consignment on security of the value of the oil.

## 147 *IG* II² 903[1]

Even in Athens, oil was sometimes in short supply. Such a shortfall could be caused by warfare or harvest failure. In 175–174 BC Athens was hit by a shortage of oil. An oil merchant, whose name has not survived, came to the rescue of the city.

The Gods (be with us). Callimachus, from the deme of Paeania, proposed: since [name lost] being involved in maritime trade and wishing to increase the income of the people as much as possible, sailed into Piraeus, in the year that Hippias was *archon* (chief civil magistrate) (181–180 BC) and sold grain to the city for a fair price. And subsequently, in the year that Hippacus was *archon* (176–175 BC), [the same man], having bought 1,500 *metretai* of oil in [. . .] which he planned to import into Pontus, taking on board there grain as a return cargo to bring to Piraeus, observed during his stay in our cities that there was a severe shortage of oil, due to harvest failure in our territory. And as he wanted to show his goodwill towards the people in every possible manner, he hastened to convey into our *emporion* the oil he had bought. And after the oil had been conveyed out of the *emporion*, our *agoranomoi* (magistrates in charge of supervision of the market) approached him, to present [the oil to the city, and when they suggested a price below] the one he asked, [. . .] he had the heart to sell[. . . .]

*NOTE*

1 New text established by P. Gauthier, *REG* 95 (1982), 275–90.

## 148 *SEG* XV 108

In AD 121 the emperor Hadrian, in his capacity as Athenian magistrate, issued a decree, valid only for Athens, according to which producers had to sell a set proportion of their yearly produce to the state. This law clearly shows the importance of oil for the Athenian economy.

Oil producers shall deliver one-third or, if owners of the Hipparchus estates sold by the fiscus, one-eighth, for only the latter estates have this advantage. They shall make delivery in instalments at the beginning of the harvest, in proportion to the amount being harvested, and they shall [give it] to the *elaionai* (oil officials) who look out for the [public requirements]. They shall file with [the *elaionai* and] the herald (of the Council and Demos) [a declaration as to the amount and character] of the harvest and hand over two [copies] and get [one copy back] with an endorsement. The declaration shall be made under oath and shall contain a statement as to how much was harvested altogether and through the slave so-and-so or the freedman so-and-so and whether the owner of the estate or the producer of the oil-jobber is to sell the crop.

The exporter shall file with the same officials a declaration stating how much he is offering for sale and to whom and where the ship is anchored. Whoever has [sold] for export without having filed a declaration, even if he has delivered to the city what he owed her, shall suffer confiscation of the stock he has agreed to sell.

Whoever has made false declarations either concerning what was harvested or what was being exported or the estate, i.e. if anyone has bought from the fiscus property other than that of Hipparchus and has delivered only one-eighth, he shall suffer confiscation of the stock and the informant shall receive one half.

[. . .] export of undeclared [. . .] the [. . .] himself or whoever [. . .] shall [. . .] and he shall keep half the purchase money, if he has not yet handed it over, or shall receive half the purchase money; the other half of the purchase money shall be confiscated.

Also the shipper shall declare that he is exporting and how much from each source. And if he is caught sailing off without having filed a declaration, he shall suffer confiscation of the oil; and if he has already sailed and is then informed against, a suit shall be filed with his city of origin and with me by the Demos (of the Athenians).

The council alone shall judge the cases concerning these matters up to the amount of fifty amphorae, and above this amount together with the Demos. If the informer is one of the crew, the (hoplite) general must convoke a meeting of the council on the morrow, or a meeting of the Assembly if the case brought by the informer is for more than fifty amphorae. And half shall be given to the informer if he proves the charge.

If anyone demands trial either in my court or in that of the proconsul, the Demos (of the Athenians) shall elect syndics.

In order that the penalties against transgressors be strictly imposed, the oil shall be delivered to the public treasury at the local market price. If from an abundance of oil at any time the amounts of one-third and one-eighth being deposited are in excess of the public requirements for the whole year, it shall be permitted as follows to those who have not as yet delivered either all or part of their oil. First they shall make out a second declaration stating, in respect to a public share owed at that time, how much it is that the *elaionai* and the *argyrotamiai* (treasurers) do not want to accept from them, which, on the one hand, they owe [. . .].

(trans. Oliver)

# 11 Building materials

Transport was a costly affair in the ancient world, especially over land (see text no. 170). One would therefore expect ancient cities to procure heavy products such as building materials from the nearest possible source. It seems, however, that few if any communities in the ancient world were fully self-sufficient in this respect, and building materials were among the more important cargoes after grain.

The demand for wood (used for construction works, for shipbuilding and also to meet energy needs) often could not be met locally. For the construction of the Minoan and the Mycenaean palaces, wood, especially cedar-wood from the Lebanon, was imported on a large scale. The Athenian demand for wood for its ambitious building projects, and of course for the fleet, was enormous. Athens' main suppliers were Asia Minor and Macedonia. In the Hellenistic and Roman periods wood was often in short supply locally, and had to be imported over long distances. The huge demand of Rome could only partly be met from Italian sources like Latium, Etruria and Umbria, which served as a source of firewood. The Lebanon, Cyprus and Calabria were also suppliers of building materials.

### 149 Theophrastus, *Plant-researches* IV.5.5

Theophrastus (*c*. 370–288 BC), the successor to Aristotle, wrote a treatise about different species of plants, in which he points out that not all varieties of wood were equally suitable for shipbuilding.

Again it is only a narrow extent of country which produces wood fit for shipbuilding at all, namely in Europe the Macedonian region, and certain parts of Thrace and Italy; in Asia Cilicia, Sinope and Amisus, and also the Mysian Olympus, and Mount Ida; but in these parts it is not abundant. For Syria has Syrian cedar, and they use this for their galleys.

### 150 Plato, *Critias* 111c

The demand for wood for different purposes could also have serious effects on the environment. Plato comments that the huge demand of Athens for wood has led to the large-scale deforestation of Attica, once covered by forests.

At that time the land, being unimpaired, contained mountains and high hills; and the plains, which are now called Phellei, were covered with rich soil, and there was abundant timber on the mountains, of which traces may still be seen. For some of our mountains at present provide only food for bees, but not so very long ago trees fit for the roofs of vast buildings were felled there, and the rafters are still in existence. There were also many other lofty cultivated trees which provided unlimited fodder for beasts.

### 151 Xenophon, *Hellenica* VI.1.11

Wood was an essential resource, and for the Greek cities it was of strategic importance to secure a sufficient supply. In 374 BC Polydamas, from Pharsalus in Thessaly, suggests to the Spartans that they occupy Macedonia. He is keenly aware of the difficulties which this would cause the Athenians:

'To see whether my calculations are reasonable', he said, 'consider these points also. With Macedonia in our possession, the place from which the Athenians get their timber, we shall of course be able to construct far more ships than they. Again, who are likely to be better able to supply these ships with men, the Athenians or ourselves, who have so many serfs of so excellent a sort? And who are likely to be better able to maintain the sailors, we, who on account of our abundance even have corn to export to other lands, or the Athenians, who have not even enough for themselves unless they buy it?'

(trans. Brownson)

### 152 Strabo IV.6.2

Liguria, an area in northern Italy, was famous for its wood, which was particularly suitable for shipbuilding. The geographer Strabo describes how this wood was marketed in Genoa, in exchange for other products.

This country is occupied by the Ligures, who live on sheep, for the most part, and milk, and drink made of barley; they pasture their flocks in the districts next to the sea, but mainly in the mountains. They have there in very great quantities timber that is suitable for ship-building, with trees so large that the diameter of their thickness is sometimes found to be eight feet. And many of these trees, even in the variegation of the grain, are not inferior to the thyme wood for the purposes of table-making. These, accordingly, the people bring down to the emporium of Genoa, as well as flocks, hides and honey, and receive, therefor a return-cargo of olive oil and Italian wine (the little wine they have in their country is mixed with pitch, and harsh).

(trans. Jones)

The ancient demand for building materials, and especially for marble, was enormous. For their building programme of the fifth and fourth centuries BC, the Athenians got their marble partly from such nearby sources as Pentelicom and Hymettus, and partly from more remote suppliers such as the islands of Naxos, Paros and Chios, and Ephesus in Ionia. In the Hellenistic period cities like Alexandria and Pergamum, as well as Athens, formed the background for many building activities. These activities necessitated large-scale imports of building materials. Exotic varieties of marble were in particularly strong demand. One of the main centres of production was the area of Nicomedia in Bithynia.

### 153 Strabo XII.8.14

In the Roman period the largest demand for building materials came from the city of Rome itself. Strabo describes the effects of this demand on the small city of Synnada in Asia Minor, famous for its colourful variety of marble.

Synnada is not a large city; but there lies in front of it a plain planted with olives, about sixty stadia in circuit. And beyond it is Docimaea, a village, and also the quarry of 'Synnadic' marble (so the Romans call it, though the natives call it 'Docimite' or 'Docimaean'). At first this quarry yeilded only stones of small size, but on account of the present extravagance of the Romans great monolithic pillars are taken from it, which in their variety of colours are nearly like the alabastrite marble; so that, although the transportation of such heavy burdens to the sea is difficult, still, both pillars and slabs, remarkable for their size and beauty, are conveyed to Rome.

(trans. Jones)

# 12 Slaves

A peculiar sort of commerce was formed by the slave trade. Chattel-slavery was a widespread phenomenon in antiquity, and slaves were employed, sometimes alongside free labour, in nearly all economic sectors.

### 154 Herodotus V.6

Many slaves were home-bred, but a constant supply of new slaves was needed. The main external sources of slaves were warfare and piracy, but others existed; poor parents sometimes exposed the children whom they could not maintain, in the expectation that they would be found and raised as slaves. Sometimes we even hear of certain foreign tribes who thought very little about selling their children into slavery. Herodotus mentions the Thracians in this connection:

The rest of the Thracians carry on an export trade in their own children; they exercise no control over young girls, allowing them to have connexions with any man they please; their wives, on the other hand, whom they purchase at high prices from their parents, they watch very strictly.

(trans. De Sélincourt)

### 155 Philostratus, *Life of Apollonius* VIII.7.12

Philostratus points out that the Phrygians sold their relatives abroad, and he maintains that Greeks would never do such a thing.

For although one can buy here on the spot slaves from Pontus or Lydia or Phrygia, indeed you can meet whole droves of them being conducted hither, since these like other barbarous nations have always been subject to foreign masters, and as yet see nothing disgraceful in servitude; the Phrygians are even accustomed to sell off their children, and once they are enslaved, they never think any more about them. The Greeks, on the contrary, love freedom, and no Greek will ever sell a slave out of his country; for which reason kidnappers and slave-dealers never resort thither, least of all to Arcadia; for in addition to the fact that they are beyond all other Greeks jealous of liberty, they also require a great number of slaves themselves.

### 156 Aristophanes, *Wealth* 501–27

In Aristophanes' comedy *Plutus* (Wealth), a certain Chremylus imagines an ideal world. He is reminded, however, by the goddess *Penia* (Poverty) of the necessity to work. Chremylus disagrees; as he sees it, there will always be a large supply of Thessalian slaves.

*Chremylus*: The present state of our human life can only be described as utter madness and lunacy. Many wicked men live in prosperity through their ill-gotten gains, while others of great virtue are poor and hungry and always accompanied by *you*. So I say again that if Wealth recovers his sight and puts an end to all this, this is the surest way to bring the greatest benefits to all men.

*Poverty*: You two old men are certainly very easily persuaded to lose your wits! You're real members of the Stuff and Nonsense Club! If what you desire were to happen, it would by no means be to your advantage. If Wealth were to see once more and divide himself in fair shares to all, no one would pursue any trade or craft any more. And with no trades or crafts, who'll do your metalwork? Who'll build your ships? Who'll be your tailors, your turners, your cobblers, your brickmakers, your launderers, your tanners? Who'll break up the clods with his plough and harvest the fruits of the Goddess of Corn, if it's open to him to forget about all that and live in idleness?

*Chremylus*: What rubbish you talk! All those things you mentioned, why, our slaves will do them for us.

*Poverty*: And where will you get your slaves from?

*Chremylus*: Buy them, of course.

*Poverty*: But why should anyone sell them, if he's already got all the money he wants?

*Chremylus*: Oh, say a merchant coming from Thessaly, where all the kidnappers are, to sell them at a profit.

*Poverty*: But on the plan *you're* putting forward, there just won't *be* any kidnappers. If a man's rich, why should he want to risk his life doing something like that? So you see, you'll have to do all your own ploughing and digging and all the other back-breaking work. You'll have an even more miserable life than now.

(trans. Sommerstein)

### 157 Strabo XIV.5.2

Warfare was a major source of slaves. After a battle, or after the capture of a city, it was accepted practice to take prisoners of war and to take them home as slaves. The process whereby Rome established its domination over the Mediterranean involved the displacement of tens of thousands of former enemies to the slave estates of southern Italy. Another important source was piracy. Although ancient states often claimed that they wanted to free the seas of the activities of pirates, they also appreciated their role as regular suppliers of slaves. The pirates of Cilicia, on the southern shore of Asia Minor, were notorious for their activities as slave traders, until Pompey put an end to their activities in 67 BC. They marketed their merchandise in the slave market on the island of Delos.

The first place in Cilicia, then, to which one comes, is a stronghold, Coracesium, situated on an abrupt rock, which was used by Diodotus, called Tryphon, as a base of operations at the time when he caused Syria to revolt from the kings and was fighting it out with them, being successful at one time and failing at another. Now Tryphon was hemmed up in a certain place by Antiochus, son of Demetrius, and forced to kill himself; and it was Tryphon, together with the worthlessness of the kings who by succession were then reigning over Syria and at the same time over Cilicia, who caused the Cilicians to organise their gangs of pirates; for on account of his revolutionary attempts others made like attempts at the same time, and thus the dissensions of brethren with one another put the country at the mercy of any who might attack it. The exportation of slaves induced them most of all to engage in their evil business, since it proved most profitable; for not only were they easily captured, but the market, which was large and rich in property, was not extremely far away, I mean Delos, which could both admit and send away ten thousand slaves on the same day; whence arose the proverb, 'Merchant, sail in, unload your ship, everything has been sold.' The cause of this was the fact that the Romans, having become rich after the destruction of Carthage and Corinth, used many slaves; and the pirates, seeing the easy profit therein, bloomed forth in great numbers, themselves not only going in quest of booty but also trafficking in slaves.

(trans. Jones)

### 158 J. Roger, *Revue Archéologique*, 6th series, 24 (1945), 49 no. 3

The funerary stèlè of a first-century AD slave trader from Amphipolis in northern Greece shows on a small relief a row of eight slaves, chained together at the neck. A striking detail is that the slave trader was an ex-slave.

Aulus Caprilius Timotheus, freedman of Aulus, slave trader.

### 159 *TAM* V.2 932

Not all slave traders had a similarly low status, however. An association of slave traders from Thyatira in Lydia honoured a colleague who had performed the minor magistracy of *agoranomos*.

The dealers in the slave market and the agents handling slaves have honoured Alexander, son of Alexander, slave merchant who has acted scrupulously during the four months in which he has been *agoranomos*: and they have set up this statue. He has presented largesses to the city from his own resources, in a most generous way, during the days of the festivals of the *Augusti* (the emperors).

# 13 Trade with the Orient and the barbarians

The Mediterranean region represents a unity in many respects. It is a landlocked sea, surrounded by mountainous areas, and its population is largely concentrated on a relatively narrow strip of coastal plains. Hardly any ancient city was located very far from the sea, which resulted in ease of communication and a considerable degree of mobility of people and resources. The unity of the Mediterranean region was reinforced by Alexander the Great and his successors, who brought a common form of Hellenism to the eastern part, and by the Romans, who eventually brought the entire region under a single political system.

### 160 Strabo XI.2.3

The world beyond the frontiers of the Empire was little known, or not known at all. There were, however, some trading contacts. The north was only of limited interest: trade between the Greeks and the Romans and the barbarians of northern and central Europe was concentrated in the port of trade Tanaïs at the mouth of the river Don.

On the river and the lake is an inhabited city bearing the same name, Tanaïs; it was founded by the Greeks who held the Bosporus. Recently, however, it was sacked by King Polemon because it would not obey him. It was a common emporium, partly of the Asiatic and the European nomads, and partly of those who navigated the lake from the Bosporus, the former bringing slaves, hides, and such other things as nomads possess, and the latter giving in exchange clothing, wine, and the other things that belong to civilised life.

(trans. Jones)

### 161 Diodorus Siculus V.22–3

Other products of the northern trade included amber and tin. Amber could be imported from the area of Poland over land to the port of Aquileia. Diodorus

Siculus (first century BC) mentions Britain and other parts of north-western Europe as sources of amber and tin.

The inhabitants of Britain who dwell about the promontory known as Belerium are especially hospitable to strangers and have adopted a civilized manner of life because of their intercourse with merchants of other peoples. They it is who work the tin, treating the bed which bears it in an ingenious manner. This bed, being like rock, contains earthy seams and in them the workers quarry the ore, which they then melt down and cleanse of its impurities. Then they work the tin into pieces the size of knuckle-bones and convey it to an island which lies off Britain and is called Ictis; for at the time of ebb-tide the space between this island and the mainland becomes dry and they can take the tin in large quantities over to the island on their wagons. (And a peculiar thing happens in the case of the neighbouring islands which lie between Europe and Britain, for at flood-tide the passages between them and the mainland run full and they have the appearance of islands, but at ebb-tide the sea recedes and leaves dry a large space, and at that time they look like peninsulas.) On the island of Ictis the merchants purchase the tin of the natives and carry it from there across the Strait to Galatia or Gaul; and finally, making their way on foot through Gaul for some thirty days, they bring their wares on horseback to the mouth of the river Rhone.

. . . we shall now discuss the electron, as it is called (amber). Directly opposite the part of Scythia which lies above Galatia there is an island out in the open sea which is called Basileia. On this island the waves of the sea cast up great quantities of what is known as amber, which is to be seen nowhere else in the inhabited world . . . for the fact is that amber is gathered on the island we have mentioned and is brought by the natives to the opposite continent, and that it is conveyed through the continent to the regions known to us, as we have stated.

(trans. Oldfather)

Trade with other exotic areas beyond the frontiers produced equally exotic merchandise: from east Africa came ivory and wild animals, and from the deserts of the Near East precious stones. The southern parts of Arabia exported frankincense and myrrh.

The trade with India was perhaps the most important of all Roman commercial contacts beyond the frontier. Products of the Far East had always been known. For centuries, Greek traders had maintained contacts with Arabian and Indian merchants, but only on a very small scale. The expedition of Alexander the Great, and pioneering voyages like that of Eudoxus of Cnidus in 116 BC had extended knowledge of these remote parts.

From the first century BC Greek and Roman traders knew how to use the monsoons.

## 162 Strabo II.5.12

When Egypt became a Roman province trade with India increased strongly.

Again, since the Romans have recently invaded Arabia Felix with an army, of which Aelius Gallus, my friend and companion, was the commander, and since the merchants of Alexandria are already sailing with fleets by way of the Nile and of the Arabian Gulf as far as India, these regions also have become far better known to us of today than to our predecessors. At any rate, when Gallus was prefect of Egypt, I accompanied him and ascended the Nile as far as Syene and the frontiers of Ethiopia, and I learned that as many as one hundred and twenty vessels were sailing from Myos Hormos to India, whereas formerly, under the Ptolemies, only a very few ventured to undertake the voyage and to carry on traffic in Indian merchandise.

(trans. Jones)

## 163 Strabo XVII.1.13

The starting-point for trade with India was Alexandria, which profited greatly by the trade with the Orient.

Among the happy advantages of the city, the greatest is the fact that this is the only place in all Egypt which is by nature well situated with reference to both things – both to commerce by sea, on account of the good harbours, and to commerce by land, because the river easily conveys and brings together everything into a place so situated – the greatest emporium in the inhabited world.

(trans. Jones)

## 164 Pliny, *Natural History* VI.104–6

From Alexandria traders went up the Nile in river craft to Coptus. They travelled over land from Coptus to the ports of Myos Hormos or Berenice on the Red Sea, where they finally embarked for India.

Travelling by sea begins at midsummer before the dogstar rises or immediately after its rising, and it takes about thirty days to reach the Arabian port of Cella or Cane in the frankincense-producing district. There is also a third port named Muza, which is not called at on the voyage to India, and is only used by merchants trading in frankincense and Arabian perfumes. . . . But the most advantageous way of sailing to India is to set out from Ocelis; from that port it is a forty days' voyage, if the Hippalus (westerly wind) is blowing, to the first trading-station in India, Muziris – not a desirable port of call, on account of the neighbouring pirates, who occupy a place called Nitriae, nor is it specially rich in articles of merchandise; and furthermore the roadstead for shipping is a long way from the land, and cargoes have to be brought in and carried out in boats. . . . Travellers set sail from India on the return voyage at the beginning of the Egyptian month Tybis, which is our December, or at all events before the sixth day of the Egyptian Mechir, which works out at before January 13 in our calendar – so making it possible to return home in the same year. They set sail from India with a south-east wind, and after entering the Red Sea, continue the voyage with a south-west or south wind.

(trans. Rackman – adapted)

### 165 *Periplus Maris Erythraei* 41–5

The intensity of the trade between Egypt and India is perhaps best illustrated by the *Periplus of the Erythraean Sea*, a first-century manual for traders who sailed between Egypt and India. The author, who was probably a shipper himself, presents a detailed description of the west coast of India.

Immediately after the gulf of Barake is the gulf of Barygaza and the coast of the region of Ariake, the beginning both of Manbano's realm and of all of India. The part inland, which borders on Skythia, is called Aberia, the part along the coast Syrastrene. The region, very fertile, produces grain, rice, sesame oil, ghee, cotton, and the Indian cloths made from it, those of ordinary quality. There are a great many herds of cattle, and the men are of very great size and dark skin color. The metropolis of the region is Minnagara, from which great quantities of cloth are brought to Barygaza. In the area there are still preserved to this very day signs of Alexander's expedition, ancient shrines and the foundations of encampments and huge wells. The voyage along the coast of this region, from Barbarikon to the promontory near Astakapra across from Barygaza called Papike, is 3,000 stades.

Beyond it is another gulf, on the inside of the waves, that forms an inlet directly to the north. Near the mouth is an island called Baiones, and, at the very head, a mighty river called the Mais. Vessels whose destination is Barygaza cross the gulf, which is about 300 stades wide, leaving the island, whose highest point is visible, to the left and heading due east toward the mouth of Barygaza's river. This river is called the Lamnaios.

This gulf which leads to Barygaza, since it is narrow, is hard for vessels coming from seaward to manage. For they arrive at either its right-hand side or its left-hand, and attempting it by the left-hand side is better than the other. For, on the right-hand side, at the very mouth of the gulf, there extends a rough and rock-strewn reef called Herone, near the village of Kammoni. Opposite it, on the left-hand side, is the promontory in front of Astakapra called Papike; mooring here is difficult because of the current around it and because the bottom, being rough and rocky, cuts the anchor cables. And, even if you manage the gulf itself, the very mouth of the river on which Barygaza stands is hard to find because the land is low and nothing is clearly visible even from nearby. And, even if you find the mouth, it is hard to negotiate because of the shoals in the river around it.

For this reason local fishermen in the king's service come out with crews [sc. of rowers] and long ships, the kind called *trappaga* and *kotymba*, to the entrance as far as Syrastrene to meet vessels and guide them up to Barygaza. Through the crew's efforts, they maneuver them right from the mouth of the gulf through the shoals and tow them to predetermined stopping places; they get them under way when the tide comes in and, when it goes out, bring them to anchor in certain harbors and basins. The basins are rather deep spots along the river up to Barygaza. For this lies on the river about 300 stades upstream from the mouth.

All over India there are large numbers of rivers with extreme ebb-and-flood tides that at the time of the new moon and the full moon last for up to three days, diminishing during the intervals. They are much more extreme in the area around Barygaza than elsewhere. Here suddenly the sea floor becomes visible, and certain parts along the coast, which a short while ago had ships sailing over them, at times become dry land, and the rivers, because of the inrush at flood tide of a whole concentrated mass of seawater, are driven headlong upstream against the natural direction of their flow for a good many stades.

(trans. Casson)

## 166 *P. Vind.* G. 40822[1]

The organization of the trade with India is illustrated by a unique papyrus from the second century AD. This contains an agreement between two parties, concerning the transport of a cargo from Muziris in India to Myos Hormos or

Berenice under a maritime contract. The loan had to be paid back after the return voyage. The papyrus is not the contract for the maritime loan, but a secondary contract, which spells out the consequences of failing to pay off the loan.

. . . of your other agents and managers. And I will weigh and give to your cameleer another twenty talents for loading up for the road inland to Coptus, and I will convey [sc. the goods] inland through the desert under guard and under security to the public warehouse for receiving revenues at Coptus, and I will place [them] under your ownership and seal, or of your agents or whoever of them is present, until loading [them] aboard at the river, and I will load [them] aboard at the required time on the river on a boat that is sound, and I will convey [them] downstream to the warehouse that receives the duty of one-fourth at Alexandria and I will similarly place [them] under your ownership and seal or of your agents, assuming all expenditures for the future from now to the payment of one-fourth – the charges for the conveyance through the desert and the charges of the boatmen and for my part of the other expenses.

With regard to there being – if, on the occurrence of the date for repayment specified in the loan agreements at Muziris, I do not then rightfully pay off the aforementioned loan in my name – there then being to you or your agents or managers the choice and full power, at your discretion, to carry out an execution without due notification or summons.

You will possess and own the aforementioned security and pay the duty of one-fourth, and the remaining three-fourths you will transfer to where you wish and sell, re-hypothecate, cede to another party, as you may wish, and you will take measures for the items pledged as security in whatever way you wish, sell them for your own account at the then prevailing market price, and deduct and include in the reckoning whatever expenses occur on account of the aforementioned loan, with complete faith for such expenditures being extended to you and your agents or managers and there being no legal action against us [in this regard] in any way. With respect to [your] investment, any shortfall or overage [sc. as a result of the disposal of the security] is for my account, the debtor and mortgager . . . .

(trans. Casson)

*NOTE*

1 Published and translated by L. Casson in: *ZPE* 84 (1990), 195.

The trade with India provided Rome with Chinese silk, with Indian gems and ivory, and above all with spices. Pepper (black and white) was imported in large quantities. In Rome there were special storehouses, the *horrea piperataria*, which could contain thousands of pounds of pepper. Roman products were not very attractive to the East. Roman merchants exported some glass and wine, but the bulk of the exchange was paid for in precious metals. Ancient authors believed that this unequal balance of trade caused a drain of gold from Rome to the Orient. The elder Pliny supplies some figures.

### 167 Pliny, *Natural History* XII.84

And by the lowest reckoning India, China and the Arabian peninsula take from our empire 100 million sesterces every year – that is the sum which our luxuries and our women cost us; for what fraction of these imports, I ask you, now goes to the gods or to the powers of the lower world?

(trans. Rackman)

### 168 Pliny, *Natural History* VI.101

And it will not be amiss to set out the whole of the voyage from Egypt, now that reliable knowledge of it is for the first time accessible. It is an important subject, in view of the fact that in no year does India absorb less than fifty million sesterces of our empire's wealth, sending back merchandise to be sold with us at a hundred times its prime cost.

(trans. Rackman)

# Part III

# Transport and means of transportation

# 14 The costs of ancient transport

We are ill informed about the exact costs of transport in the ancient world. Literary sources do not often quote prices, and when they do, they are not always reliable.

As in other pre-industrial societies, transport in the ancient world relied on wind and muscle power. As a result, transport, in particular transport by land, was slow and expensive. Transport by water was preferred, wherever possible.

## 169 Cato, *On Agriculture* XXII.3

When ancient authors mention the prices of certain products, they do not normally distinguish between cost price and freight rates, and it is difficult to separate the two. An exception is Cato the Elder. In his agricultural manual, Cato gives us the price of an olive press, which he breaks down further:

> A mill is bought near Suessa for 400 sesterces and fifty pounds of oil. The cost of assembling is sixty sesterces, and the charge for transportation by oxen, with six day's wages of six men, drivers included, is seventy-two sesterces . . . . At Pompeii one is bought complete for 384 sesterces, freight rate 280 sesterces.

The Price Edict provides valuable insight into the price structures of the early fourth century. It is, in fact, our main piece of evidence concerning transportation costs. Transport over land was much more expensive than transport by sea. The Edict allows us to calculate the effect of the different means of transportation on the price. Transporting a 550-kg load of grain 100 miles over land increased the price by 56 per cent; transporting the same load over the same distance by sea from Alexandria to Rome would result in an increase of only 2 per cent.

The Edict does not give the costs of river transport, but we can deduce from a first-century papyrus that river transport resulted in a price increase of 2 to 6 per cent. Modern estimates use for the average price increase as a result of the different modes a ratio of 1 (sea transport): 4.9 (river transport): 28 (land transport). These are averages of course: local difficulties (for example, the occurrence of piracy and highway robbery) and climatic circumstances could result in strong fluctuations.

## 170 *Price Edict* XVII 3–5[1]

*Land transport*

Concerning the freight rates of land transport
Freight for a 1,200 pound wagon load per mile 20 denarii
Freight for a 600 pound camel load per mile 8 denarii
Freight for an ass load per mile 4 denarii

*NOTE*

1 Based on the text of S. Lauffer, *Diokletians Preisedikt*, Berlin 1971.

## 171 *Price Edict* XXXVII.1–42[1]

*Sea transport*

Freight rates between places and provinces which it is absolutely forbidden to exceed

| | |
|---|---|
| from Alexandria to Rome | for 1 castrensis modius 16 denarii |
| from Alexandria to Nicomedia | for 1 castrensis modius 12 denarii |
| from Alexandria to Byzantium | for 1 castrensis modius 12 denarii |
| from Alexandria to Dalmatia | for 1 castrensis modius 18 denarii |
| from Alexandria to Aquileia | for 1 castrensis modius 24 denarii |
| from Alexandria to Africa | for 1 castrensis modius 10 denarii |
| from Alexandria to Sicily | for 1 castrensis modius 10 denarii |
| from Alexandria to Ephesus | for 1 castrensis modius 8 denarii |
| from Alexandria to Thessalonica | for 1 castrensis modius 12 denarii |
| from Alexandria to Pamphylia | for 1 castrensis modius 6 denarii |
| likewise from *Oriens* to Rome | for 1 castrensis modius 18 denarii |
| from *Oriens* to Salona | for 1 castrensis modius 16 denarii |
| from *Oriens* to Aquileia | for 1 castrensis modius 22 denarii |
| from *Oriens* to Africa | for 1 castrensis modius 16 denarii |
| from *Oriens* to Spain | for 1 castrensis modius 20 denarii |
| from *Oriens* to Baetica | for 1 castrensis modius 22 denarii |
| from *Oriens* to Lusitania | for 1 castrensis modius 26 denarii |
| from *Oriens* to the Gauls | for 1 castrensis modius 24 denarii |
| from *Oriens* to Byzantium | for 1 castrensis modius 12 denarii |
| from *Oriens* to Ephesus | for 1 castrensis modius 10 denarii |

| | |
|---|---|
| from *Oriens* to Sicily | for 1 castrensis modius 16 denarii |
| likewise from Asia to Rome | for 1 castrensis modius 16 denarii |
| from Asia to Africa | for 1 castrensis modius 8 denarii |
| from Asia to Dalmatia | for 1 castrensis modius 12 denarii |
| likewise from Africa to Rome | |
| from Africa to Salona | for 1 castrensis modius 18 denarii |
| from Africa to Sicily | for 1 castrensis modius 6 denarii |
| from Africa to Spain | for 1 castrensis modius 8 denarii |
| from Africa to the Gauls | for 1 castrensis modius 4 denarii |
| from Africa to Achaia | for 1 castrensis modius 12 denarii |
| from Africa to Pamphylia | for 1 castrensis modius 14 denarii |
| . . . to Sicily | for 1 castrensis modius 6 denarii |
| . . . to Thessalonica | for 1 castrensis modius 18 denarii |
| . . . to Achaia | for 1 castrensis modius 14 denarii |
| . . . to Spain | for 1 castrensis modius 10 denarii |
| . . . to the Gauls | for 1 castrensis modius 4 denarii |
| . . . to the Gauls | for 1 castrensis modius 8 denarii |
| likewise from Nicomedia to Rome | for 1 castrensis modius 18 denarii |
| from Nicomedia to Ephesus | for 1 castrensis modius 6 denarii |
| from Nicomedia to Thessalonica | for 1 castrensis modius 8 denarii |
| from Nicomedia to Achaia | for 1 castrensis modius 8 denarii |
| from Nicomedia to Salona | for 1 castrensis modius 14 denarii |

*NOTE*

1 Text based on S. Lauffer, *Diokletians Preisedikt*, Berlin 1971.

### 172 *BGU* III 802, col. 22

A papyrus from AD 42 gives the rates for transport on the Nile between the Arsinoite nome and Alexandria. The freight rate is not the same for different cargoes.

267,897 1/2 artabas wheat
a freight rate of 2,330 artabas wheat

34,848 1/2 artabas barley
a freight rate of 198 artabas barley

5,407 artabas lentils
a freight rate of 17 1/4 artabas lentils

# 15 Transport over land

In the thousand years or so between the archaic period and the Later Empire there was little change in the means of transportation. Porters carried heavy loads in harbours, storehouses and markets. Mules were the most important category of pack animal that could also be used in less accessible, mountainous areas. Draught animals, especially oxen, were in use for heavier loads, but their disadvantage was that they were considerably slower. Horses were less used as draught animals than in other pre-industrial periods because the ancient way of harnessing horses was less efficient.

### 173 *IG* II² 1673

Oxen were also used for extremely heavy loads such as building materials. Fourth-century building accounts from Eleusis provide information on the transport of huge pieces of stone, of more than 5 tonnes each, which were destined for the new portico:

We began to bring a column drum . . . . it was brought in three days; thirty-one yokes of oxen transported it. We began to bring another drum . . . . thirty-three yokes transported it; it was brought in three days.

We began to bring another drum . . . . twenty-seven yokes transported it on the first day; on the second day were added three; it was brought in three days.

We began to bring two drums at one time on a double rig on the tenth of the month; forty yokes transported them on the first day, on the second were added five; they were brought in two and a half days.

Two types of vehicle were in use throughout antiquity: ox-carts for the transport of heavy loads, and lighter vehicles pulled by mules (and, less usually, horses) for the conveyance of passengers.

We have little information about different types of vehicles used during the Greek period, but we know of a wide variety from the Roman period. Passenger vehicles ranged from light two-wheeled chariots to large coaches. Among the lighter two-wheeled vehicles were the *essedum*, which was a luxurious vehicle in use by officials, and the *cisium* and the *covinnus*, which were simpler small vehicles for single travellers with little luggage. The Romans also adapted the Etruscan *carpentum*, a cabriolet drawn by a span of mules. The *carruca* was a larger four-wheeled wagon capable of carrying four passengers and a coachman. The largest vehicle in this category was the *raeda*, which was drawn by two or four horses and which showed some resemblance to the stage-coach of later periods.

Heavier vehicles were in use for the transportation of agricultural produce to and from the farms, and of other goods to and from the towns. In most cases different types of ox-cart were used. The *plaustrum* was the most common type in use by farmers. Another similar model which the sources mention is the *sarracum*, which was heavier, and had closed wheels, making it especially suitable for the transportation of building materials. The *carrus* and the *clabula* were used by the army to transport goods and personnel over long distances.

## 174 *Theodosian Code* VIII.5.30

Information about the exact carrying capacity of individual types of vehicle before the Later Empire is hard to find. An imperial decree from AD 368 informs us of the regulations covering vehicles in use by the *cursus clabularis*, a transport service charged with the duty of furnishing provisions for the army, created by Septimius Severus.

Emperors Valentinian, Valens, and Gratian, Augusti, to Viventius, Praetorian Prefect.

We clearly sanctioned that in the wagonbeds of carriages no one should exceed the measure prescribed below, that is, no person should dare to place a burden of more than one thousand pounds on a carriage, or more than one thousand five hundred pounds on a post wagon, or more than thirty pounds on a posthorse.

Therefore, We have delivered written instructions to the Illustrious masters of the horse and foot that they should station watchful and diligent members of the imperial bodyguard throughout the places which should be furnished with guards for the enforcement of this regulation, so that they may always inspect the size of the vehicles and the amount of the loads and may not allow anything to be done contrary to this law.

Furthermore, if any person should be found to have exceeded the limits prescribed by this law, by the excessive size either of his vehicle or of the burden, no matter what class or high rank he may allege, or how much the burden is proved to have exceeded the statutory limit, he shall be detained in the custody of the imperial bodyguard who detected such arrogance, until a reference to Our Clemency may be dispatched with respect to said person who held Our interdict in contempt.

(trans. Pharr)

### 175 *Theodosian Code* VIII.5.17

The same emperors also issued a decree in AD 364 in which they prohibited the construction of very large vehicles.

Emperors Valentinian and Valens Augusti, to Menander.

We shall allow nothing beyond a thousand pounds of weight to be placed on vehicles, and thus couriers shall be satisfied that We grant them the right to transport thirty pounds on their horses. Therefore, if it should be established that any load exceeds this measure, the excess must be confiscated to the fisc, at the expense of the person who committed this offense against the law.

We also decree that it shall be sanctioned that the use of enormous vehicles shall entirely cease, so that if any workman should suppose that he might make a vehicle beyond the norm that We have prescribed, he shall not doubt that if he is free, he must undergo the punishment of exile; if a slave, perpetual punishment by labor in the mines.

(trans. Pharr)

### 176 S. Mitchell, *JRS* 66 (1976), 109

The burden of providing transport for the use of civilian and military officials of the Roman Empire and for the carriage of supplies and provisions fell mainly on the subject population. A long series of imperial documents, stretching from the first to the early fifth century AD, records the practice of requisitioning transport. A first-century AD inscription from Sagalassus in Pisidia is the first of this series.

Sextus Sotidius Strabo Libuscidianus, *legatus pro praetore*[1] of Tiberius Caesar Augustus, says:

It is the most unjust thing of all for me to tighten up by my own edict that which the Augusti, one the greatest of gods, the other the greatest of emperors, have taken the utmost care to prevent, namely that no-one should make use of carts without payment. However, since the indiscipline of certain people requires an immediate punishment, I have set up in the individual towns and villages a register of those services which I judge ought to be provided, with the intention of having it observed, or, if it shall be neglected, of enforcing it not only with my own power but with the majesty of the best of princes from whom I received instructions concerning these matters.

The people of Sagalassus must provide a service of ten wagons and as many mules for the necessary uses of people passing through, and should receive, from those who use the service, ten *asses* per *schoenum* for a wagon and four *asses* per *schoenum* for a mule, but if they prefer to provide donkeys, should give two in place of one mule at the same price. Alternatively, if they prefer, they can pay people of another town or village who undertake the duty the same price for individual mules and wagons as they would have received if they had provided the service themselves, in order that these perform the same service. They are obliged to provide transport as far as Cormasa and Conana.

However, the right to use this service will not be granted to everyone, but to the procurator of the best of princes and his son, and they are granted the use of up to ten wagons, or three mules in place of a single wagon or two donkeys in place of a single mule on the same occasion, being liable to pay the price that I have decided. In addition (use of the service is granted) to persons on military service, both to those who have a diploma,[2] and to those who travel through from other provinces on military service in the following manner: no more than ten wagons, or three mules for individual wagons, or two donkeys for individual mules, should be provided to senators of the Roman people being liable to pay the sum I have prescribed; three wagons, or three mules for individual wagons, or two donkeys for individual mules, must be provided to a Roman knight whose services are being employed by the best of princes on the same condition, but if anyone requires more he shall hire them at a price decided by the person who hires them out; a wagon, or three mules, or six donkeys, shall be provided to a centurion on the same condition.

I want nothing to be provided for those who transport grain or anything else of that sort either for their own use or to sell, and (nothing should be provided) for anyone for their own personal baggage animals or for their freedmen's or for their slaves' animals. Shelter and hospitality should be provided without payment for all members of my own staff, for persons on military service from other provinces and for freedmen and slaves of the best of princes and for the animals of these persons, in such a way that these do not exact other services without payment from people who are unwilling.

(trans. Mitchell)

## *NOTES*

1 Governor of the province Galatia. Pisidia was in the beginning of the first century AD a part of that province. The governor was the second highest-ranking official in the province. He had special responsibilities for provisioning and supplying both troops and officials.

2 They received their authorization from the provincial governor, whose name and official seal, required in the *diploma*, would be familiar to the local inhabitants and a sufficient guarantee of the document's authority.

# 16 The roads

In classical Greece no *polis* was very far from the sea, and transport between towns was largely effected by sea. Roads were often no more than small tracks through mountainous areas, accessible only to pedestrians and pack-animals. Even the larger roads that led to some of the larger sanctuaries were not always accessible to vehicles.

More elaborate road systems were found in large states, such as the Persian and the Roman empires. These roads were not primarily designed to facilitate commercial exchange, but served as an instrument of power, enabling the authorities to control subject territories.

## 177 Herodotus V.52–3

The Persian kings constructed a large number of well-kept roads, which enabled them to maintain communication with even the more remote parts of the Persian empire. The most famous of these was, of course, the Royal Road between Sardis, in Lydia, and the Persian capital, Susa, a distance of 1,600 miles. Royal messengers were able to travel this distance in twenty days, but other travellers needed around one hundred days.

At intervals all along the road are recognized stations, with excellent inns, and the road itself is safe to travel by, as it never leaves inhabited country. In Lydia and Phrygia, over a distance of ninety-four and a half parasangs – about 330 miles – there are twenty stations. On the far side of Phrygia one comes to the river Halys; there are gates here, which have to be passed before one crosses the river, and a strong guard-post. Once over the river and into Cappadocia, a distance of 104 parasangs, with twenty-eight stations, brings one to the Cilician border, where the road passes through two sets of gates, both guarded. These left behind, the distance through Cilicia is fifteen and a half parasangs, with three stations. Separating Cilicia from Armenia is a river, the Euphrates, which has to be crossed in a boat, and the distance across Armenia itself is fifty six and a half parasangs, with fifteen stations or stopping-places. Here, too, there is a guard. Through this part of the country four rivers run, all of which have to be crossed by a ferry: the first is the Tigris; the second and third both have the same names – Zabatus – though they are different rivers and flow from distinct sources, one rising in Armenia, the other in Matiene; and the fourth is the Gyndes – the river which Cyrus once split up into 360 channels. Leaving Armenia and entering Matiene, one has 137 parasangs to go, with thirty-four stations, and, passing from thence into Cissia, another forty-two and a half with eleven stations, which bring one to the river Choaspes – another navigable stream – on which the city of Susa stands. Thus the total number of stations, or posthouses, on the road from Sardis to Susa is 111. If the measurement of the Royal Road in parasangs is correct, and if a parasang is equal (as indeed it is) to thirty furlongs, then the distance from Sardis to the Palace of Memnon (450 parasangs) will be 13,500 furlongs. Travelling, then, at the rate of 150 furlongs a day, a man will take just ninety days to make the journey. So one can see that Aristagoras of Miletus was quite right when he told the Spartan Cleomenes that it took three months to reach Susa from the sea. But, if anyone wants still greater accuracy, I would point out that the distance from Ephesus to Sardis should be added to the total, so that one gets, as a final measurement of the distance from the Aegean to Susa – the 'city of Memnon' – 14,040 furlongs, Ephesus to Sardis being 540 furlongs, which increase the three months' journey by three days.

(trans. De Sélincourt)

**178 Pausanias VIII.6.4–6**

The roads in Greece were of a very different character. Pausanias, the author of a second-century AD description of Greece, describes the state of the roads which led into the isolated region of Arcadia on the central Peloponnese.

There is one way into Arcadia from the territory of Argos near Hysiae across Mount Parthenium into the territory of Tegea, and a second and third by Mantinea, through the so-called Prinus, and by 'the Ladder'. This last way is broader, and the road down has steps that were once cut in it. . . . The remaining route is narrower and goes by Artemisium.

## 179 Pausanias VIII.54.5

Not all roads were as bad as that:

The road to Argos from Tegea is very well suited to carriages, mostly a first-rate highway. First of all on this road there is a shrine and statue of Asclepius. Later if you head off left for 200 yards there is a collapsed sanctuary of Pythian Apollo, utter ruins. Along the straight road there are a lot of oak-trees; there is a shrine of Demeter in the sacred oak-wood called Demeter of the Corytheans, and nearby another sanctuary of mystic Dionysus. It is from this point that Mount Parthenium begins.

The Romans paid much more attention to the construction of roads and highways than did the Greeks. During the Republic, the Roman authorities started the construction of a system of highways which made possible communication between Rome and the different parts of its Empire. The *Via Flaminia* went from Rome over the Apennines to Fanum Fortunae (Fano) on the Adriatic coast. The *Via Aemilia* established connection with Placentia (Piacenza) and Mediolanum (Milan). Along the west coast the *Via Aurelia* led from Rome to Luna.

## 180 Strabo V.3.8

. . . for if the Greeks had the repute of aiming most happily in the founding of cities, in that they aimed at beauty, strength of position, harbours, and productive soil, the Romans had the best foresight in those matters which the Greeks made but little account of, such as the construction of roads and aqueducts, and of sewers that could wash out the filth of the city into the Tiber. Moreover, they have so constructed also the roads which run throughout the country, by adding both cuts through hills and embankments across valleys, that their wagons can carry boat-loads.

(trans. Jones)

## 181 Plutarch, *Gaius Gracchus* 7

The tribune Gaius Gracchus (123 BC) paid a lot of attention to the construction of roads.

His roads were planned so as to run right across the country in a straight line, part of the surface consisting of dressed stone and part of tamped-down gravel. Depressions were filled up, any watercourses or ravines which crossed the line of the road were bridged, and both sides of the road were levelled or embanked to the same height, so that the whole of the work presented a beautiful and symmetrical appearance. Besides this he had every road measured in miles – the Roman mile is a little less than eight furlongs – and stone pillars erected to mark the distances. Other stones were set up at shorter intervals on both sides of the road so that horsemen should be able to mount from these without help.

(trans. Scott-Kilvert)

### 182 Statius, *Silvae* IV.40–55

The construction of the *Via Domitiana* at the end of the first century AD is described by the poet Statius.

The first task here is to trace furrows, ripping up the maze of paths, and then excavate a deep trench in the ground. The second comprises refilling the trench with other material to make a foundation for the road build-up. The ground must not give way, nor must bedrock or base be at all unreliable when the paving stones are trodden. Next the road metalling is held in place on both sides by kerbing and numerous wedges. How numerous the squads working together! Some are cutting down woodland and clearing the higher ground, others are using tools to smooth outcrops of rock and plane great beams. There are those binding stones and consolidating the material with burnt lime and volcanic tufa. Others again are working hard to dry up hollows that keep filling with water, or are diverting the smaller streams.

### 183 Procopius, *Histories* V.147

Most famous of all Roman highways was the 'Queen of roads' (*Regina viarum*), the *Via Appia*, which led south to Capua and hence to Brundisium (Brindisi). It dated back to the fourth and third centuries BC. It needed occasional repairs, but in the sixth century the Byzantine historian Procopius could still admire its solid construction. To this day the *Via Appia* is a symbol of Rome's achievements in civil engineering.

The Appian Way is five days in length for a well-trained traveller: for it extends from Rome to Capua. And the breadth of the road is such that two wagons going in opposite directions can pass one another; it is one of the most notable sights of the world. For Appius quarried all the stone, which is mill-stone and hard by nature, elsewhere far away, and brought it there, for it is not found anywhere in this district. And after making those stones smooth and flat and cutting them to a polygonal shape, he fastened them together without putting concrete or anything else between them. And they were fixed so well and the points were so firmly closed, that spectators get the impression that they are not fitted together, but grown together. And now after the passage of so long a time and being traversed by many wagons and animals every day, they have neither separated at all at the joints, nor has any of the stones worn out or become less thick. Nay, they have not even lost any of their polish. Such, then, is the Appian Way.

### 184 *CIL* III 7203

The state of the highways was a major concern of the emperors. We know this not only from literary sources, but also from numerous inscriptions which were set up in different parts of the Empire. The following inscription was found near Smyrna in Asia Minor.

The Emperor Caesar Vespasian Augustus, *pontifex maximus*, holding the tribunician power for the sixth year (AD 75), acclaimed *imperator* thirteen times, father of his country, consul six times, designated consul for a seventh time, censor, saw to the repair of the roads.

### 185 *CIL* III 8267

In AD 100 the emperor Trajan constructed a road on the right bank of the Danube.

The Emperor Caesar Nerva Trajan Augustus Germanicus, son of the deified Nerva, *pontifex maximus*, holding the tribunician power for the fourth year, father of his country, consul three times, built this road by cutting through mountains and eliminating the curves.

### 186 Galen, *On Methods of Healing* X.632–3

The achievements of Trajan were mentioned by Galen, a medical author of the second century AD.

[E]ven today we see that some of the ancient highways of the world are in part swampy, in part covered by stones or thickets; that they are difficultly steep or dangerously sloping, infested with wild animals, impassable because of the width of the rivers, long, or rough. Yet all the roads in Italy in this condition Trajan improved. In the parts that were marshy and swampy he spread layers of stones or elevated the roadbed with high fills; he cleared away the rough and thorny sections and built bridges over impassable points on the rivers; where the road was unduly long he constructed a short cut in another place; for example, if the road was difficult because of the steepness of the hill he deflected it through more accessible regions; if it was infested with wild animals or deserted he diverted its course, directing it through populated districts and smoothing the rough patches as well.

(trans. Frank)

### 187 Strabo IV.6.6

Despite these efforts, it was not possible to overcome every problem. Especially in mountainous areas, travellers ran up against many difficulties.

For in addition to his putting down the brigands Augustus Caesar built up the roads as much as he possibly could; for it was not everywhere possible to overcome nature by forcing a way through masses of rock and enormous beetling cliffs, which sometimes lay above the road and sometimes fell away beneath it, and consequently, if one made even a slight misstep out of the road, the peril was one from which there was no escape, since the fall reached to chasms abysmal. And at some places the road there is so narrow that it brings dizziness to all who travel it afoot – not only to men, but also to all beasts of burden that are unfamiliar with it; the native beasts, however, carry the burdens with sureness of foot. Accordingly, these places are beyond remedy; and so are the layers of ice that slide down from above – enormous layers, capable of intercepting a whole caravan or of thrusting them all together into the chasms that yawn below; for there are numerous layers resting one upon another, because there are congelations upon congelations of snow that have become ice-like, and the congelations that are on the surface are from time to time easily released from those beneath before they are completely dissolved in the rays of the sun.

(trans. Jones)

### 188 Ammianus Marcellinus XV.10.3–5

Ammianus Marcellinus describes the dangerous journey through the Alps between northern Italy and southern Gaul.

In these Cottian Alps, which begin at the town of Susa, there rises a lofty ridge, which scarcely anyone can cross without danger. For as one comes from Gaul it falls off with sheer incline, terrible to look upon because of overhanging cliffs on either side, especially in the season of spring, when the ice melts and the snows thaw under the warmer breath of the wind; then over precipitous ravines on either side and chasms rendered treacherous through the accumulation of ice, men and animals descending with hesitating step slide forward, and wagons as well. And the only expedient that has been devised to ward off destruction is this: they bind together a number of vehicles with heavy ropes and hold them back from behind with powerful efforts of men or oxen at barely a snail's pace; and so they roll down a little more safely. And this, as we have said, happens in the spring of the year. But in winter the ground, caked with ice, and as it were polished and therefore slippery, drives men headlong in their gait and the spreading valleys in level places, made treacherous by ice, sometimes swallow up the traveller. Therefore those that know the country well drive projecting wooden stakes along the safer spots, in order that their line may guide the traveller in safety. But if these are covered with snow and hidden, or are overturned by the streams running down from the mountains, the paths are difficult to traverse even with natives leading the way.

(trans. Rolfe)

**189 *CIL* I 206 lines 56–67**

Ancient towns had narrow streets and were not designed for heavy traffic. The enormous growth of Rome during the second and first centuries BC led to many traffic problems. The noise and dangers of urban traffic were well known, and led to some attempts to regulate the flow of traffic in Rome. The *Lex Julia Municipalis* of 45 BC had attempted to relieve Rome of at least some of its wheeled transport during the day:

In the roads which are or shall be within the city of Rome, or within the limit of continuous habitation, no person, after the first day of January next following, shall be allowed in the daytime, after sunrise or before the tenth hour of the day, to lead or drive any heavy wagon; except where it shall be requisite, for the sake of building the sacred temples of the immortal gods or carrying out some public work, to draw or convey material into the city, or where, in pursuance of a contract for the demolition of buildings, it shall be requisite for public ends to carry material out of the city or away from such places, and in cases and for objects for the which it shall be lawful for specified persons and for specified causes to lead or drive such wagons.

On all days when the Vestal Virgins, the *rex sacrorum*, and the *flamines* (priests) shall be required to ride in wagons in the city for the sake of the public sacrifices of the Roman people, or when wagons shall be required for a triumphal procession on the day fixed for such triumph, or for games which shall be publicly celebrated within the city of Rome or within one mile of the city, or for the procession at the Circus Games, for all such causes and on all such days it shall be lawful for wagons to be led or driven in the city in the daytime, notwithstanding any enactments in this law.

It shall be lawful for wagons, brought into the city by night, drawn by oxen or horses, if returning empty or conveying away refuse, to be in the city of Rome or within one mile of the city after sunrise in the first ten hours of the day, notwithstanding any enactments in this law.

(trans. Hardy – adapted)

# 17 River transport

### 190 Strabo IV.1.14

Transport over land was inconvenient and expensive, and travellers and traders preferred the routes over sea and along rivers. In Gaul river transport was an integral part of trade. The whole of that country was well supplied with rivers, but the rivers were not always navigable, and transport over land could not always be avoided. Strabo describes how the Rhône becomes unnavigable in the Lyon area:

But since the Rhône is swift and difficult to sail up, some of the traffic from here goes by land on wagons, that is all the traffic to the Arvernians and to the river Loire, although the Rhône in its course draws close to these also; but the fact that the road is level and only 800 stades, is an invitation not to sail upstream, since it is easier to go by land. From here the road is in a natural way succeeded by the Loire.

### 191 Pliny, *Letters* X.41.1–2

Occasionally farsighted officials suggested digging canals in order to improve communications, but such plans rarely succeeded. Pliny's idea of connecting a lake in Asia Minor (the Sabanja lake) with the sea underlines the awareness of transport costs in the Roman Empire, but was never executed.

In consideration of your (sc. Trajan) noble ambition which matches your supreme position, I think I should bring to your notice any projects which are worthy of your immortal name and glory and are likely to combine utility with magnificence. There is a sizeable lake not far from Nicomedia, across which marble, farm produce, wood, and timber for building are easily and cheaply brought by boat as far as the main road; after which everything has to be taken on to the sea by cart, with great difficulty and increased expense. To connect the lake with the sea would require a great deal of labour, but there is no lack of it. There are plenty of people in the countryside, and many more in the town, and it seems certain that they will all gladly help with a scheme which will benefit them all.

(trans. Melmoth)

### 192 Tacitus, *Annals* XIII.53.2–4

In AD 55 the imperial legate in the province of Germania Superior, L. Antistius Vetus, entertained the idea of constructing a canal between the Moselle and the Saône, but his colleague in the province of Gallia Belgica managed to dissuade him.

Up to now, Germany had been peaceful because, prodigal awards having cheapened the honorary Triumph, our generals looked for greater glory from maintaining peace. To keep the troops busy, the imperial governor of Lower Germany, Pompeius Paulinus, finished the dam for controlling the Rhine, begun sixty-three years previously by Nero Drusus. His colleague in Upper Germany, Lucius Antistius Vetus, planned to build a Saône–Moselle canal. Goods arriving from the Mediterranean up the Rhône and Saône would thus pass via the Moselle into the Rhine, and so to the North Sea. Such a waterway, joining the western Mediterranean to the northern seaboard, would eliminate the difficulties of land transport. But the imperial governor of Gallia Belgica, Aelius Gracilis, jealously prevented his neighbour in Lower Germany from bringing his army into the province he governed. 'This would be currying favour in Gaul, and would worry the emperor,' he objected – using an argument which often blocks good projects.

### 193 *P. Erasm.* II 50

A variety of vessels sailed the river Nile. The *kerkouros* was the largest type; it was used to transport grain downstream to Alexandria, whence it was exported. In many texts the capacity and the actual cargo are mentioned. A recently published papyrus from 149 BC mentions a *kerkouroskaphe*. Normally this term refers to a small ship, but in this case a ship with a fairly large capacity is meant.

Year 32, 11 Pachon, 1026 ½ artabas of wheat.

Year 32, 11 Pachon. Kephalon, *naukleros* of the *kerkouroskaphe* of Eubulus, with a capacity of 4,000 (artabas), declares that he had loaded, in the harbour at Kaine, the destination being the royal granary at Alexandria, from the harvest of the 32nd year, from Theon, the *sitologos*[1] of the *ergasterion* (workshop) at Oxyrrhyncha: one thousand twenty-six and a half artabas of tax wheat, total 1,026 ½ (artabas), (measured out) with the *dochikon*-measure which has been calibrated on the basis of the bronze standard, and (levelled off) with the straight strickle, and I have no claims on you.

## *NOTE*

1 A royal official in charge of grain revenues and supplies.

# 18 Transport by sea

In classical antiquity two basic types of merchantmen existed. Galleys were used for cargo that required rapid transport. Smaller types were almost completely dependent on oars, the square sail being used only under very favourable conditions. Larger galleys used oars only when entering or leaving a harbour. On the high seas they used sails.

Several specialized varieties of this type existed: the *phaselus* was used for passenger transport, the *akatos* (Latin: *actuarius*) for cargo, and the *keles* (Latin: *celox*) for extra-fast transport.

Most ships were real sailing ships (in Greek: *strongylon ploion* or *holkas*, in Latin: *navis oneraria*). Maritime archaeologists have shown that some of these ships were more than 40 metres long and may have had a capacity of 400 tons. The smaller types carried a mainsail; the larger ones also a topsail and/or a foresail. The larger types had two or three masts. These ships did not need to remain close to the coast, nor did they require special harbour facilities.

Finally, there were some super-freighters with a capacity of more than 1,000 tons. They were used only for the transport of building materials and grain for the *annona* and could anchor only in the large ports of Ostia, Alexandria, Antioch, Massilia, Carthage and Piraeus.

### 194 Homer, *Odyssey* II.418–28

Homer's descriptions of the Greek ships bear a strong resemblance to the representations of ships on Geometric vases of the eighth century BC. These were fast and open galleys, with a small foredeck, and a larger poop deck. Sizes differed: the 20-oared *eikosoros* was used for troops; the 50-oared *pentekonter* was used for the transport of goods. According to Homer's description, most ships were black, and had curved stem- and stern-posts.

The sailors cast the hawsers off, climbed in, and took their places on the benches. And now, out of the West Athena of the flashing eyes called up for them a steady following wind and sent it singing over the wine-dark sea. Telemachus shouted to the crew to lay hands on the tackle and they leapt to his orders. They raised the fir mast, set it inside the hollow *mesodme* (carlings to hold the mast) and fastened it down with the forestays. They drew up the white sails with well-braided thongs. Struck full by the wind, the sail swelled out, and a dark wave hissed loudly round her stem as the vessel gathered way.

(trans. Rieu – adapted)

**195 Thucydides I.10.4**

Homer's description of the crossing of the Greek fleet to Troy was commented upon by Thucydides a couple of centuries later:

. . . if we can here also accept the testimony of Homer's poems, in which, without allowing for the exaggeration which a poet would feel himself licensed to employ, we can see that it was far from equalling ours. He has represented it as consisting of twelve hundred vessels; the Boeotian complement of each ship being a hundred and twenty men, that of the ships of Philoctetes fifty. By this, I conceive, he meant to convey the maximum and the minimum complement: at any rate he does not specify the amount of any others in his catalogue of the ships. That they were all rowers as well as warriors we see from his account of the ships of Philoctetes, in which all the men at the oar are bowmen. Now it is improbable that many supernumeraries sailed if we except the kings and high officers; especially as they had to cross the open sea with munitions of war, in ships, moreover, that had no decks, but were equipped in the old piratical fashion.

(trans. Crawley)

**196 Plutarch, *Pericles* XXVI.3–4**

In the sixth century BC the inhabitants of the island of Samos put to sea an exceptionally large *pentekonter* for the transport of heavy loads.

The *Samaina* is a ship boar-prowed at the nose and bigbellied and roomy so that it can sail in open water and serve as a fast galley of the line. It was so called because it made its first appearance at Samos, where the tyrant Polycrates had built some.

**197 Athenaeus V.206d–209b**

An exceptionally large ship, equipped with every kind of luxury, was the *Syracusia*, which was launched by the tyrant Hiero II of Syracuse in c. 240 BC. He did not enjoy his ship for long, if we can believe the story of Athenaeus. When Hiero discovered that the ship was too large to moor in most harbours round the Mediterranean, he made a present of it to King Ptolemy III Euergetes (246–221 BC) of Egypt.

I cannot refrain from mentioning the ship built by Hiero of Syracuse, the one supervised by Archimedes the mathematician, since there is an account of it published by a certain Moschion which I recently read over carefully. Here is what Moschion writes:

'Hiero, . . . eager to gain a reputation in the field of shipbuilding, had a number of grain-carriers built, the construction of one of which I shall describe. For the materials, he collected timber from Mt. Etna, enough to build 60 quadriremes; then, partly from Italy and partly from Sicily, the wood for treenails, the upper and lower parts of the frames, and other elements; for cordage, esparto from Spain and hemp and pitch from the Rhône Valley; and the rest of his needs from a variety of places. He recruited carpenters and other craftsmen, chose one of them, Archias of Corinth, to be foreman, pressed him to set right to work, and gave the project his personal attention daily. Since there were three hundred craftsmen, exclusive of assistants, working on the materials, half of the ship was finished in six months, down to the sheathing of each area, as it was completed, with lead sheets. He gave orders to launch this portion so that the rest of the work could be carried out afloat. After much discussion of how the launching should be done, Archimedes, the engineer, carried it out by himself along with a handful of assistants. He constructed a screw-windlass which drew that huge craft down to the sea.[1] The rest of the ship took another six months; the whole hull was pinned together with copper spikes, most of which weighed ten pounds and some fifteen.[2]

'Once the exterior was finished, work began to the interior. The vessel, though built after the model of a "twenty-er", had three levels of gangways. The lowest, reached by numerous companionways, was for working cargo. The next was designed to give access to the cabins. The next – the highest – was for the men-at-arms aboard. At the middle level, along both sides of the ship, were the cabins for the men, thirty in all and each of four-couch size. The owner's cabin was of fifteen-couch size with three cubicles of three-couch size; the kitchen aft was for these. All had floors done in multicolored mosaic; in these was worked, in amazing fashion, the whole story of the *Iliad*. Trim, overheads, and doors were all carefully worked. Along the uppermost gangway was a gymnasium, as well as promenades built to suit a vessel of this size. These had marvelously flourishing plant beds of all kinds, which were watered through covered lead tiles; there were also arbors of white ivy and grapes whose roots, planted in big jars filled with soil, were watered in the same way as the flower beds. The arbors provided shade along the promenades. Alongside these was a chapel to Aphrodite, three-couch size, whose floor was paved with agate and other of the most decorative stones found on the island of Sicily. The bulkheads and overhead were of cypress, and the doors of ivory and aromatic cedar. It was beautifully fitted out with paintings, statues, and utensils for libations. Next to it was a reading room, five-couch size, with bulkheads and doors of boxwood, a library, and, in the overhead, a circular concavity made to look like the sundial at Achradina. There was also a bath, three-couch size, with three copper tubs and a fifty-gallon basin made of the colored stone of Tauromenium. There were, in addition, accommodations for passengers and the bilge-watchers. Furthermore, there were ten stables along each side, which also held the fodder for the horses and the gear of the riders and grooms. There was a sealed watertank in the bows with a capacity of 20,000 gallons, made of planks and waterproofed fabric. Alongside it was a sealed fishtank made of planks and sheets of lead; it was filled with seawater, and a good supply of fish was kept alive in it. On each side of the vessel, beams jutted out, spaced the same distance apart; these supported woodbins, ovens, stoves, millstones, and other services. All around the ship ran a series of exterior *atlantes*,[3] nine feet high and spaced equally apart, which supported the uppermost parts of the deck structures and the triglyph; moreover, the whole ship was decorated with suitable paintings.

'There were eight towers, of the same height as the deck-structures of the ship: two aft, the same number forward, and the rest amidships. Each was fitted with two booms ending in open platforms through which stones could be hurled down on any enemy that sailed underneath. On each tower were stationed four heavily armed young marines and two archers. The insides of the towers were crammed with stones and missiles. Across the ship ran a battlemented parapet surrounding a raised fighting deck that rested on pillars; on this was set a catapult capable of throwing a 180-lb. stone or an eighteen-foot dart; the instrument had been designed by Archimedes. Its range with either missile was 200 yards. Nearby were protective screens joined by thick leather straps and hung from bronze chains. Each of the three masts was fitted with two booms for dropping missiles; from these, grappling hooks or chunks of lead could be hurled down on an enemy. All around the ship ran an iron palisade as protection against boarding attempts; there were also grappling irons fired by catapult, which could seize an enemy ship and pull it alongside for a mortal blow. Sixty fully armed young marines were stationed along each side of the vessel and an equal number around each mast with its booms for dropping missiles. There were also men in the mast-tops, which were made of bronze: three were assigned to the main [literally "first mast"], and two and one to the other two respectively. Slaves hauled up stones and darts to the mast-top parapets by means of baskets on lines running over blocks.

'There were four anchors of wood and eight of iron. When it came to the timber for the masts, the fore and mizzen were found easily enough, but the main was located only with great difficulty in the mountains of Bruttium by a man from Sybotis; Phileas of Tauromenium, the engineer, had it hauled down to the shore. Although the bilge was extraordinarily deep, it was bailed by only one man using a screw-pump, one of Archimedes' inventions.

'The name of the ship was the *Syracusia* ["The Syracuse"] but, when Hiero sent it off, he changed it to the *Alexandris* ["The Alexandria"]. As ship's boats it had, first a *kerkouros*[4] of 3,000 talents burden [= seventy-eight tons] with a full complement of oars, then some *haliades*[5] of half that burden, and, in addition, a good number of small boats. The total complement was no less than [number lost]; over and above all mentioned so far, there were 600 stationed forward to carry out any orders. Crimes committed aboard ship were brought before a court consisting of the owner, captain, and first mate, who judged in accordance with the laws of Syracuse.

'The vessel was loaded with 60,000 measures of grain, 10,000 jars of pickled Sicilian fish, 20,000 talents of wool, and 20,000 talents of miscellaneous cargo; in addition, there were the provisions for the crew. When Hiero heard that, of all the harbors it was to call at, some would not accommodate the ship at all and others were risky, he decided to send it as a gift to King Ptolemy in Alexandria, since there was a shortage of grain in Egypt at the time. He did so, the ship arrived at Alexandria, and docked there.'

(trans. Casson)

*NOTES*

1 Archimedes was the first to discover and construct the screw-windlass.
2 These were made fast to the ribs, being fitted into holes bored through, and then were covered over by the underlayer of tarred fabric and overlayer of lead sheeting that protected the planking.
3 Male caryatids.
4 The standard grain-carrier on the Nile.
5 Dispatch boats on the Nile.

### 198 Lucian, *The Ship* 5

The ships that were used for the transport of grain were perhaps less luxuriously equipped, but they were still quite impressive. Lucian describes the amazement caused by the arrival of the grain ship *Isis*, which had sought shelter in Piraeus.

According to the ship's carpenter, the ship was 120 cubits in length, the beam more than a quarter of that, and from the deck to the bottom, to the lowest point in the bilge, twenty-nine cubits. And then the height of the mast, and what a yard it carried, and what a forestay it held up. And the way the stern rose up in a gentle curve ending in a gilded goose-head, matched at the other end by the forward, more flattened, sweep of the prow with the figure of Isis, the goddess the ship was named after, on each side. The rest of the decoration, the paintings, the red topsail, even more, the anchors with their capstans and winches, and the stern cabins, everything was incredible. The crew was like an army. They told me she carried enough grain to feed Athens for a year. And one little old man, who turns those great steering oars with a tiller that is no more than a stick, was responsible for its safety.

### 199 Pliny, *Natural History* XVI.201–2

The obelisk that now stands in St Peter's Square was brought to Rome during the reign of Caligula. A special ship was constructed for the transport of the obelisk, which weighs 322 tons, and its base, weighing 174 tons. The mainmast of the ship was made of an exceptionally large pine-tree.

An especially wonderful fir was seen in the ship which brought from Egypt at the order of the emperor Gaius the obelisk erected in the Vatican Circus and four shafts of the same stone to serve as its base. It is certain that nothing more wonderful than this ship has ever been seen on the sea: it carried one hundred and twenty bushels of lentils for ballast, and its length took up a large part of the left side of the harbour of Ostia, for under the emperor Claudius it was sunk there, with three moles as high as towers erected upon it that had been made of Pozzuoli cement for the purpose and conveyed to the place. It took four men to span the girth of this tree with their arms.

(trans. Rackman)

### 200 Flavius Josephus, *My Life* 15

These very large freighters also served for the transport of passengers. The apostle Paul came to Rome on a ship like this (see text no. 217). A contemporary of Paul's, the Jewish historian Flavius Josephus, also travelled on a freighter; he was shipwrecked in the Adriatic.

I reached Rome after being in great danger at sea. For our ship was wrecked in the midst of the Adriatic Sea, and we, some 600 in all, had to swim the whole night. About daylight, through God's good providence, a ship of Cyrene appeared and I and certain others, about eighty, outstripped the others and were taken on board.

# 19 Construction

Our knowledge of ancient methods of shipbuilding is almost entirely derived from the results of underwater archaeology. Mediterranean shipbuilders started from the outside, in contrast to the prevailing methods in north-western Europe, which started with the skeleton. First the keel was laid, to which the prow and the stern were attached. Then a temporary frame was made to give the ship its proper shape. The most labour-intensive job was the construction of the shell. Starting from the keel, the planks were closely joined by mortises and tenons. Only after the hull was finished was the temporary frame removed and a final skeleton inserted to make the shell rigid. A deck or decks were added, and the steering oar, the oars, the mast, the sail and the rigging completed the construction. There is no ancient text to provide us with a complete technical treatise on ship-building, but literary texts provide some interesting details.

### 201 Homer, *Odyssey* V.244–55

The earliest literary description of the construction of a ship is also one of the most informative texts. After a sojourn of ten years on the island of Calypso, Odysseus is finally allowed to leave. Immediately he starts to build himself a boat.

He felled twenty trees in all, and adzed them with the bronze tool. He cleverly planed them and made them straight to the line. Then Calypso brought drills and he dulled them all and fitted them to each other. He hammered the ship with dowels and joints. As broad a bottom as a good shipwright will lay out for a wide merchantman, so broad a bottom did Odysseus fashion for his wide boat. He worked away setting up decks by fastening them to close set frames and finished up with the long pieces.

## 202 *P. Flor.* I 69[1]

Another important document for Greco-Roman shipbuilding is a record of payments to shipwrights and sawyers working on a boat of considerable size in the months Phaophi (28 September to 27 October) and Hathyr (28 October to 26 November) of an unspecified year in the middle of the third century AD. This text is a clear illustration of the day-to-day activities on an ancient shipyard.

(Phaophi) (day) 17: to six shipwrights for work on the aforementioned boat, at 7 drachmas each, 42 drachmas

to two sawyers for cutting persea wood, at 8 drachmas each, 16 drachmas

(day) 18: to five shipwrights for work etc., at 7 drachmas each, 35 drachmas

to two sawyers for cutting persea wood, at 8 drachmas each, 16 drachmas

(day) 19: to four shipwrights for work etc., at 7 drachmas each, 28 drachmas

to two sawyers for cutting persea wood, at 8 drachmas each, 16 drachmas

(day) 21: to five shipwrights for work etc., at 7 drachmas each, 35 drachmas

(day) 22: to four shipwrights for work etc., at 7 drachmas each, 28 drachmas

(day) 23: to six shipwrights for work etc., at 7 drachmas each, 42 drachmas

(day) 24: to four shipwrights for work etc., at 7 drachmas each, 28 drachmas

(day) 27: to seven shipwrights for work etc., at 7 drachmas each, 49 drachmas

Hathyr (day) 1: to four shipwrights for work etc., at 7 drachmas each, 28 drachmas

to two sawyers for cutting persea wood, at 8 drachmas each, 16 drachmas

(day) 2: to five shipwrights for work etc., at 7 drachmas each, 35 drachmas

to two sawyers for cutting frames of acacia, at 8 drachmas each, 16 drachmas

(day) 3: to four shipwrights for work etc., at 7 drachmas each, 28 drachmas

to two sawyers for cutting frames of acacia, at 8 drachmas each, 16 drachmas

(day) 4: to four shipwrights for work etc., at 7 drachmas each, 28 drachmas
to two sawyers for cutting frames of acacia, at 8 drachmas each, 16 drachmas
(day) 5: to three shipwrights for work etc., at 7 drachmas each, 21 drachmas
(day) 7: to four shipwrights for dismanting the planks of the scaffold on one side of the aforementioned boat, at 7 drachmas each, 28 drachmas
to two sawyers for cutting frames of acacia, at 8 drachmas each, 16 drachmas
(day) 8: to four shipwrights for dismantling the planks of the scaffold on the other side of the aforementioned boat, at 7 drachmas each, 28 drachmas

(trans. Casson)

*NOTE*

1 Published and translated by L. Casson, 'Documentary evidence for Graeco-Roman shipbuilding (*P. Flor.* I 69)', *Bulletin of the American Society of Papyrologists* 27 (1990), 17.

## 203 Theophrastus, *Plant-researches* V.7.1–3

In his treatise on plants Theophrastus (third century BC) discusses different kinds of timber, and their suitability for ship-building.

The timbers for shipbuilding are fir, pine and cedar. For triremes and other warships fir is used because of its lightness; for merchant ships pine is used because of its resistance to decay. Some also make triremes of pine because fir is not available. In Syria and Phoenicia triremes are made of cedar because of the lack of pine. In Cyprus they use coastal pine, since this is available on the island and it seems to be superior to pine. The rest of the hull is made of these woods, but the keels of the triremes are constructed of oak to withstand hauling ashore. The keels of the merchantmen are made of pine. If the latter have to be hauled out an underlayer of oak is fitted. For smaller craft beechwood is used for the keel and in general the breastwork (of the *boros*) is made of beech.

For carpentry the oldest wood is best, provided it is not rotten, for old wood is suitable for craftsmen of all sorts. But for shipbuilding wood which is rather green must be used, because of the need for bending. The fact is that planking shows gaps when it is new, but when the ship is launched the planks absorb water, close up and become watertight, except in the case of timber which has been completely dried out. In that condition planks do not make a close joint, or not as well as they would if the wood was not completely dried out.

### 204 Strabo IV.4.1

The planks that formed the hull were joined at the edges, and caulking was apparently not necessary. However, the technique was known from foreign peoples. Herodotus (see no. 208) describes how the Egyptians used papyrus for this purpose. Caulking was also used in north-western Europe, as is shown by Strabo's description of the ships built by the Gallic tribe of the Veneti.

Because of the ebb-tides, they make their ships with broad bottoms and high sterns, and high stems; they make them of oak (of which they have plentiful supply), and this is why they do not bring together the joints of the planks but leave gaps. These they caulk with sea-weed, so that the wood may not, for lack of moisture, dry out when the ships are hauled up, because the sea-weed is naturally rather moist, whereas the oak is dry and without fat.

### 205 Pliny, *Natural History* XVI.158

In more northern areas, such as in Belgia, reeds were used instead of sea-weed.

[I]n places where it (sc. reed) grows very hard and retains a measure of viscosity, as in Belgium, it is pounded up and inserted between the joints of ships to caulk the seams, being more adhesive than tar and being more reliable for filling the seams than pitch.

### 206 *Anthologia Palatina* XI.248

To prevent leakage and rot, the seams, or even entire shells, were smeared with pitch and wax.

And when the ship had been pinned together up to the thwarts, they smeared it with the glistening sap of the pine.

### 207 Pliny, *Natural History* XVI.56

The pitch with wax scraped off seagoing ships is called 'live pitch'.

## 208 Herodotus II.96

Local shipbuilding traditions could differ widely and were usually not affected by Greek and Roman practices. Herodotus describes an Egyptian ship that was constructed with thorn-bush.

The Nile boats used for carrying freight are built of acacia [?] wood – the acacia resembles in form the lotus of Cyrene, and exudes gum. They cut short planks, about three feet long, from this tree, and the method of construction is to lay them together like bricks and through-fasten them with long spikes set close together, and then, when the hull is complete, to lay the deck-beams across on top. The boats have no ribs and are caulked from inside with papyrus. They are given a single steering-oar, which is driven down through the keel; the masts are of acacia wood, the sails of papyrus. These vessels cannot sail up the river without a good leading wind, but have to be towed from the banks; and for dropping downstream with the current they are handled as follows: each vessel is equipped with a raft made of tamarisk wood, with a rush mat fastened on top of it, and a stone with a hole through it weighing some four hundredweight; the raft and the stone are made fast to the vessel with ropes, fore and aft respectively, so that the raft is carried rapidly forward by the current and pulls the 'baris' (as these boats are called) after it, while the stone, dragging along the bottom astern, acts as a check and gives her steerage-way. There are a great many of these vessels on the Nile, some of them of enormous carrying capacity.

(trans. De Sélincourt)

## 209 Caesar, *Gallic War* III.13

During his campaign in Gaul Caesar got to know the ships of the Veneti, which were well suited to the rough conditions on the Atlantic.

They (sc. the Veneti) construct their hulls with somewhat flatter bottoms than our craft to make it easier to go through the shallow depths of low tide and over shoals; the prows and the sterns are rather high to handle the size of the waves when the sea is stormy; the ships are made throughout of oak to withstand any amount of violence and hard treatment. Beams are of timbers a foot square made fast with iron nails an inch thick, and anchors are held by iron chains instead of ropes. Their sails are of hide or of softened leather instead of canvas, possibly because they have no flax or do not know how to use it, but more likely because they think canvas will not stand up to the storms of the ocean and the violence of the winds and will not drive such heavy ships efficiently.

### 210 Caesar, *Civil War* I.54

Northern-European methods of shipbuilding were sometimes adapted by the Romans. Caesar, during his campaigns in Spain in 49 BC, found himself with a shortage of ships.

He ordered his men to build boats of the kind that his experience in Britain in previous years had taught him to make. The keel and the ribs were made first, of light wood, the rest of the hull was made of wickerwork and covered with skins.

### 211 Seneca, *Letters* LXXVII.1–2

Most freighters were equipped with a single mast, to which a yard was attached that was nearly as long as the vessel itself. This yard carried a large rectangular sail. Some ships also carried an *artemon*, a small foresail set on a foremast that slanted over the bow.

On the open sea a topsail (Greek: *sipharos*; Latin: *siparum*) was raised to improve speed. This was especially important for the *tabellariae*, the dispatch boats, which heralded the arrival of the grain fleet from Alexandria.

Today suddenly the Alexandrian *tabellariae* came into view. They are the ships which are usually sent ahead to announce that the (grain) fleet is on its way; they are called 'dispatch boats'. For the Campanians they are a welcome sight. The whole population of Puteoli stands on the quayside and, even in a big crowd of ships, they try to spot the Alexandrian ships by the type of their rigging, since they are the only ones allowed to keep the topsails raised, although all use them on the open sea. . . . The topsail stands out in the Alexandrian ships.

### 212 Pliny, *Natural History* XIX.5

Some of the larger freighters also carried a mizzen between the mainmast and the stern.

By this time we are not satisfied with sails larger than the ships, but although single trees are not big enough for the yards, nevertheless other sails are added above the yards and others besides are spread on prow and poop.

# 20 The sailing season

Sailing was a seasonal activity normally restricted to the summer months when the weather conditions were stable and when the winds were predominantly northerly. During the winter months sailing was reduced to a minimum. Scant daylight, poor visibility, clouds, and the violence of storms were the main reasons. Hesiod's suggestion of restricting sailing to the fifty days after summer solstice (see text no. 4), is not followed by other authors. They allow for a somewhat longer season.

### 213 Vegetius, *Epitome Rei Militaris* IV.39

Vegetius, the author of a fourth-century AD military handbook, gives a precise indication of the times of year at which sailing was feasible.

From the sixth day before the kalends of June (27 May) until the rising of Arcturus, that is until the eighteenth before the kalends of October (24 September), navigation is believed to be safe. . . . From then up to the third before the ides of November (11 November), navigation is uncertain. . . . From the third before the ides of November until the sixth before the ides of March (10 March) the seas are closed.

### 214 *Theodosian Code* XIII.9.3

That this was not mere theory is confirmed by a decree of the Emperor Gratian from the year AD 380. The text deals with a request made by sailors for higher pay during the winter months; Gratian turned down this request.

Thus, in the future, all petitions, that is, those about the two and one half per cent which you demand from the transport of winter cargo, shall be in abeyance.

It is Our pleasure, of course, that from the month of November navigation shall be suspended; the month of April, since it is the nearest to summer, shall be used for the acceptance of cargo. The necessity of such acceptance from the kalends of April (1 April) to the kalends of October (1 October) shall be preserved permanently; navigation, however, shall be extended to the day of the ides of the aforesaid months.

## 215 Apuleius, *Metamorphoses* XI.5 and 16

In some parts of the Mediterranean the opening of the sailing season was marked by the religious feast of the *Navigium Isidis*, probably celebrated at the beginning of March, which corresponds with the outside limit of 10 March given by Vegetius.

The day which will be the day born from this night has been proclaimed mine by everlasting religious observance; on that day, when the winter's tempests are lulled and the ocean's storm-blown waves are calmed, my priests dedicate an untried keel to the now navigable sea and consecrate it as the first fruits of voyaging. You must await this rite with an attitude both calm and reverent . . . .

There, after the images of the gods had been set in their proper places, the chief priest consecrated a ship, which was constructed with fine craftmanship and decorated all over with marvellous Egyptian pictures. He took a lighted torch, an egg, and sulphur, uttered prayers of great solemnity with reverent lips, and purified the ship thoroughly, naming it and dedicating it to the goddess. The gleaming sail of this holy barque bore an inscription woven in letters of gold, whose text renewed the prayer for prosperous navigation during the new sailing season. Now rose the mast, a round pine, high and resplendent, visible from far off with its conspicuous masthead. The stern curved in a goose-neck and flashed light from its coating of gold-leaf, and the entire hull bloomed with highly polished, pale citron-wood. Then all the people, worshippers and uninitiated alike, outdid one another in loading the ship with baskets heaped with spices and similar offerings, and on the waves they poured libations of grain-mash made with milk. When the ship was laden with generous gifts and auspicious sacrifices, it was untied from its anchor-ropes and offered to the sea, as a mild breeze arose especially for it.

(trans. Graves)

**216 Demosthenes, *Against Dionysodorus* 30**

Between November and March the sea was considered 'closed', but special circumstances could arise that required sailing: military considerations played their part, but the most common reason would have been the occurrence of a food crisis (see text no. 129). In the fourth century BC the traffic between Alexandria and Rhodes continued during the winter period. This allowed merchants to make high profits.

Sailing from Rhodes to Egypt is never interrupted and they could put the same money to work two or three times, whereas here they would have had to pass the winter and to await the good season.

# 21 The hazards of the sea

Hardly any detailed descriptions of normal sea voyages can be found in ancient literature; long descriptions almost invariably describe extraordinary crossings that were struck by storm or shipwreck.

### 217 Acts of the Apostles 27

A famous account of a shipwreck is to be found in the Acts of the Apostles. The Apostle Paul has been arrested and as a Roman citizen, has made an appeal to the Emperor. He is put on a transport from the port of Caesarea to Rome. In Paul's company was the author of the Acts, who gave a detailed description of the shipwreck near Malta.

When it was decided that we should sail for Italy, Paul and some other prisoners were handed over to a centurion named Julius, of the Augustan Cohort. We embarked in a ship of Adramyttium, bound for ports in the province of Asia, and put out to sea. Aristarchus, a Macedonian from Thessalonica, came with us. Next day we landed at Sidon, and Julius very considerately allowed Paul to go to his friends to be cared for. Leaving Sidon we sailed under the lee of Cyprus because of the head winds, then across the open sea off the coast of Cilicia and Pamphylia, and so reached Myra in Lycia.

There the centurion found an Alexandrian vessel bound for Italy and put us on board. For a good many days we made little headway, and we were hard put to it to reach Cnidus. Then, as the wind continued against us, off Salmone we began to sail under the lee of Crete, and, hugging the coast, struggled on to a place called Fair Havens, not far from the town of Lasea.

By now much time had been lost, and with the Fast already over, it was dangerous to go on with the voyage. So Paul gave them this warning: 'I can see, gentlemen, that this voyage will be disastrous; it will mean heavy loss, not only of ship and cargo but also of life.'

But the centurion paid more attention to the captain and to the owner of the ship than to what Paul said; and as the harbour was unsuitable for wintering, the majority were in favour of putting to sea, hoping, if they could get so far, to winter at Phoenix, a Cretan harbour facing south-west and north-west. When a southerly breeze sprang up, they thought that their purpose was as good as achieved, and, weighing anchor, they sailed along the coast of Crete hugging the land. But before very long a violent wind, the Northeaster as they call it, swept down from the landward side. It caught the ship and, as it was impossible to keep head to wind, we had to give way and run before it. As we passed under the lee of a small island called Cauda, we managed with a struggle to get the ship's boat under control. When they had hoisted it on board, they made use of tackle to brace the ship. Then, afraid of running on to the sandbanks of Syrtis, they put out a sea-anchor and let her drift. Next day, as we were making very heavy weather, they began to lighten the ship; and on the third day jettisoned the ship's gear with their own hands. For days on end there was no sign of either sun or stars, the storm was raging unabated, and our last hopes of coming through alive began to fade.

When they had gone for a long time without food, Paul stood up among them and said, 'You should have taken my advice, gentlemen, not to put out from Crete: then you would have avoided this damage and loss. But now I urge you not to lose heart; not a single life will be lost, only the ship. Last night there stood by me an angel of the God whose I am and whom I worship. "Do not be afraid, Paul," he said; "it is ordained that you shall appear before Caesar; and, be assured, God has granted you the lives of all who are sailing with you." So take heart, men! I trust God: it will turn out as I have been told; we are to be cast ashore on an island.'

The fourteenth night came and we were still drifting in the Adriatic Sea. At midnight the sailors felt that land was getting nearer, so they took a sounding and found twenty fathoms. Sounding again after a short interval they found fifteen fathoms; then, fearing that we might be cast ashore on a rugged coast, they let go four anchors from the stern and prayed for daylight to come. The sailors tried to abandon ship; they had already lowered the ship's boat, pretending they were going to lay out anchors from the bows, when Paul said to the centurion and the soldiers, 'Unless these men stay on board you cannot reach safety.' At that the soldiers cut the ropes of the boat and let it drop away.

Shortly before daybreak Paul urged them all to take some food. 'For the last fourteen days', he said, 'you have lived in suspense and gone hungry; you have eaten nothing. So have something to eat, I beg you; your lives depend on it. Remember, not a hair of your heads will be lost.' With these words, he took bread, gave thanks to God in front of them all, broke it, and began eating. Then they plucked up courage, and began to take food themselves. All told there were on board two hundred and seventy-six of us. After they had eaten as much as they wanted, they lightened the ship by dumping the grain into the sea.

When day broke, they did not recognize the land, but they sighted a bay with a sandy beach, on which they decided, if possible, to run ashore. So they slipped the anchors and let them go; at the same time they loosened the lashings of the steering-paddles, set the foresail to the wind, and let her drive to the beach. But they found themselves caught between cross-currents and ran the ship aground, so that the bow stuck fast and remained immovable, while the stern was being pounded to pieces by the breakers. The soldiers thought they had better kill the prisoners for fear that any should swim away and escape; but the centurion was determined to bring Paul safely through, and prevented them from carrying out their plan. He gave orders that those who could swim should jump overboard first and get to land; the rest were to follow, some on planks, some on parts of the ship. And thus it was that all came safely to land.

(*The Revised English Bible*)

### 218 Synesius, *Letters* 4

A less well-known, but not less interesting account of a sea voyage has come to us from the hand of Synesius (AD 370–413) who was to become bishop of Ptolemais in Libya. In a letter of AD 404 he writes about a turbulent journey from Alexandria to his home town in Libya. His letter is full of the prejudices of the landowning upper class against professional sailors (see also above, pp. 3–20).

*To his brother*

Although we started from Bendideum at early dawn, we had scarcely passed Pharius Myrmex by noonday, for our ship went aground two or three times in the bed of the harbour. This mishap at the very outset seemed a bad omen, and it might have been wiser to desert a vessel which had been unlucky from the very start. But we were ashamed to lay ourselves open to an imputation of cowardice from you, and accordingly 'It was no longer granted us to tremble or to withdraw'. So now, if misfortune awaits us, we shall perish through your fault.

After all, was it so dreadful that you should be laughing and we out of danger? But of Epimetheus they aver that 'His prudence was at fault, his repentance never', and that is precisely our own case, for we might easily have saved ourselves in the first instance; whereas now we are lamenting in concert on desert shores, gazing out towards Alexandria to our heart's content, and towards our motherland Cyrene; one of these places we wilfully deserted, while the other we are unable to reach, all the time having seen and suffered such things as we never thought to happen even in our dreams. Hear my story then, that you may have no further leisure for your mocking wit, and I will tell you first of all how our crew was made up. Our skipper was fain of death owing to his bankrupt condition; then besides him we had twelve sailors, thirteen in all! More than half of them, including the skipper, were Jews – a graceless race and fully convinced of the piety of sending to Hades as many Greeks as possible. The remainder were a collection of farm boys who up to last year had never gripped an oar, but the one batch and the other were alike in this, that every man of them had some personal defect. Accordingly, so long as we were in safety they passed their time in jesting one with another, accosting their comrades not by their real names, but by the distinguishing marks of their misfortunes, as to call out 'Cripple', 'Ruptured', 'Squint'. Each one had his distinguishing mark, and to us this sort of thing was no small source of amusement. The moment we were in danger, however, it was no laughing matter, but rather did we bewail these very defects. We had embarked to the number of more than fifty, about a third of us being women, most of them young and pretty. Do not, however, be too quick to envy us, for a curtain separated us from them and a stout one at that, the suspended fragment of a recently torn sail, to virtuous men the very wall of Semiramis. Nay, Priapus himself might well have been temperate had he taken passage with Amarantus, for there was never a moment when this fellow allowed us to be free from fear of the uttermost danger. As soon as he had rounded the cape, near you, with the temple of Poseidon, he made straight for Taposiris, with all sails spread, to all seeming bent upon confronting Scylla, over whom we were all wont to shudder in our boyhood when doing our school exercises. This manoeuvre we detected only just as the vessel was nearing the reefs, and we all raised so mighty a cry that perforce he gave up his attempt to battle with the rocks. All at once he veered about as though some new idea had possessed him, and went for the open water, struggling as best he might against a contrary sea.

Presently a fresh south wind springs up and carries us along, and soon we are out of sight of land and have come into the track of the double-masted freighters, whose business does not lie with our Libya; they are sailing in quite another course. Again we make common cause of complaint, and our grievance now is that we have been forced away too far from the shore. Then does this Titan of ours, Amarantus, fulminate, standing up on the stern and hurling awful imprecations upon us. 'We shall obviously never be able to fly,' he said; 'how can I help people like you who distrust both the land and the sea?' 'Nay,' I said, 'not so, worthy Amarantus, in case any one uses them rightly. For our own part we had no yearning for Taposiris, for we wanted only to live. Moreover,' I continued, 'what do we want of the open sea? Let us rather make for Pentapolis, hugging the shore; for then, if indeed we have to face one of those uncertainties which, as you admit, are unfortunately only too frequent on the deep, we shall at least be able to take refuge in some neighbouring harbour.' I did not succeed in persuading him by my talk, for to all of it the outcast only turned a deaf ear; and what is more, a gale commenced to blow from the north, and the violent wind soon raised seas mountains high. This gust falling suddenly on us, drove our sail back, and made it concave in place of its convex form, and the ship was all but capsized by the stern. With great difficulty, however, we headed her in.

Then Amarantus thunders out, 'See what it is to be master of the art of navigation. I had long foreseen this storm, and that is why I sought the open. I can tack in now, since our sea room allows us to add to the length of our tack. But such a course as the one I have taken would not have been possible had we hugged the shore, for in that case the ship would have been dashed on the coast.' Well, we were perforce satisfied with his explanation so long as daylight lasted and dangers were not imminent, but these failed not to return with the approach of night, for as the hours passed the seas increased continually in volume. Now it so happened that this was the day on which the Jews make what they term the 'Preparation', and they reckon the night, together with the day following this, as a time during which it is not lawful to work with one's hands. They keep this day holy and apart from the others, and they pass it in rest from labour of all kinds. Our skipper accordingly let go the rudder from his hands the moment he guessed that the sun's rays had left the earth, and throwing himself prostrate, 'allowed to trample on him what sailor so desired'.[1]

We who at first could not understand why he was thus lying down, imagined that despair was the cause of it all. We rushed to his assistance and implored him not to give up the last hope yet. Indeed the hugest waves were actually menacing the vessel, and the very deep was at war with itself. Now it frequently happens that when the wind has suddenly relaxed its violence, the billows already set in motion do not immediately subside; they are still under the influence of the wind's force, to which they yield and with which they battle at the same time, and the oncoming waves fight against those subsiding. I have every need of my store of flaming language, so that in recounting such immense dangers I may not fall into the trivial. To people who are at sea in such a crisis, life may be said to hang by a thread only, for if our skipper proved at such a moment to be an orthodox observer of the Mosaic law, what was life worth in the future? Indeed we soon understood why he had abandoned the tiller, for when we begged him to do his best to save the ship, he stolidly continued reading his roll. Despairing of persuasion, we finally attempted force, and one staunch soldier – for many Arabs of the cavalry were of our company – one staunch soldier, I say, drew his sword and threatened to behead the fellow on the spot if he did not resume control of the vessel. But the Maccabaean in very deed was determined to persist in his observances. However, in the middle of the night he voluntarily returned to the tiller. 'For now', he said, 'we are clearly in danger of death, and the law commands.' On this the tumult sprang up afresh, groaning of men and shrieking of women. All called upon the gods, and cried aloud; all called to mind those they loved. Aramantus alone was in good spirits, for he thought to himself that now at last he would foil his creditors. For myself, amidst those horrors, I swear to you by the god sacred to philosophy, that the only thing that troubled me was a passage from Homer. I feared that were my body once swallowed up in the waves, the soul itself also might eternally perish, for somewhere in his epic he writes: 'Ajax perished, once he had drunk of the briny wave',[2] bearing witness to the fact that death at sea is the most grievous way of perishing, for in no other case does the poet speak of annihilation, but of every one who dies the phrase is 'he went to Hades'. Thus in the two books of the Nekuiai[3] the lesser Ajax is not brought into the narrative, for this very reason, that his soul is not in Hades; and again, Achilles, the most high-spirited and the most daring of all, shrinks from death by drowning and refers to it as a pitiable ending.[4] As I was musing in this fashion, I noticed that all the soldiers on board were standing with drawn swords. I asked why and learned from them that they regarded it as more honourable to belch up their souls to the winds while still on the deck, than to gape them out to the waves. These men are by nature true descendants of Homer, thought I, and I entirely approved their view of the matter. Then someone loudly proclaimed that everyone possessing gold should suspend it about the neck, and those who possessed it did so, as well as those who had anything of the value of gold. The women themselves put on their jewellery, and distributed cords to those who needed them: such is the time-honoured custom. Now this is the reason for it. It is a matter of necessity that the corpse from a shipwreck should carry with it the fee for burial, inasmuch as whosoever comes across the dead body and profits by it, will fear the laws of Adrastia [Nemesis], and will scarcely grudge sprinkling a little sand on the one who has given to him so much more in value. So then they occupied themselves, but I sat solemnly apart, my thoughts fixed on the heavy sum of money which my host had deposited with me. I was lamenting, not so much my approaching death, the god of hospitality be my witness! as the sum of money which would be lost to this Thracian before whom, even when dying, I should feel shame. I came to the point of regarding it as a luxury to die in the fullest sense of the word, above all to perish in such a way as to escape all consciousness hereafter. Now what made death gape at our feet was the fact that the ship was running under full sail, because we could not shorten sail, for as often as we attempted this we were thwarted by the ropes, which were jammed in the blocks; and again we had a secret fear lest in the night time, even if we lived out the sea, we should approach land in this sorry plight.

But day broke before all this had time to occur, and never, I know, did we behold the sun with greater joy. The wind grew more moderate as the temperature became milder, and thus, as the moisture evaporated, we were able to work the rigging and handle sail. We were unable, it is true, to replace our sail by a new one, for this was already in the hands of the pawnbroker, but we took it in like the swelling folds of a garment, and in four hours' time we who had imagined ourselves already in the jaws of death, were disembarking in a remote desert place, possessing neither town nor farm near it, only an expanse of open country of one hundred and thirty stadia. Our ship was riding in the open sea, for the spot was not a harbour, and it was riding on a single anchor. The second anchor had been sold, and a third Amarantus did not possess. When now we touched the dearly beloved land, we embraced the earth as a real living mother. We sent up hymns of gratitude to Providence, as is our custom, and to all this we added a mention of the present good fortune by which we had been saved contrary to all expectation. Thus we waited two days until the sea should have abated its fury. When, however, we were unable to discover any way out by land, for we could find no one in the country, we decided to try our fortune again at sea. We straightway started at dawn with a wind which blew from the stern all that day and the following one, but towards the end of this second day the wind left us and we were in despair. However, only too soon should we be longing for a calm. It was the thirteenth day of the waning moon, and a great danger was now impending, I mean the conjunction of certain constellations and those well-known chance events which no one, they say, ever confronted at sea with impunity. So at the very moment when we should have stayed in harbour, we so far forgot ourselves as to run out again to sea. The storm opened with north winds and with heavy rain during the moonless night, presently the winds raged without measure, and the sea became deeply churned up. As to ourselves, exactly what you might expect at such a crisis took place. I will not dilate a second time on the identical sufferings, I will only say that the very magnitude of the storm was helpful. First the yard began to crack, and we thought of tightening up the vessel; then it broke in the middle and very nearly killed us all. It seems that this very accident, failing to destroy us, was the means of our salvation. We should never have been able to resist the force of the wind, for again the sail was intractable and defied all our efforts to take it in. Contrary to all prevision we had shaken off the rapacious violence of our enforced run, and were carried along during a day and a night, and at the second crowing of the cock, before we knew it, behold we were on a sharp reef which ran out from the land like a short peninsula. Then a shout went up, for someone passed the word that we had gone aground on the shore itself. There was much shouting and very little agreement. The sailors were terrified, whereas we through inexperience clapped our hands and embraced each other. We could not sufficiently express our great joy. And yet this was accounted the most formidable of the dangers that had beset us. Now when day appeared, a man in rustic garb signalled and pointed out which were the places of danger, and those that we might approach in safety. Finally, he came out to us in a boat with two oars, and this he made fast to our vessel. Then he took over the tiller, and our Syrian gladly relinquished to him the conduct of the ship. So after proceeding not more than fifty stadia, he brought her to anchor in a delightful little harbour, the name of which I believe is Azarium, and there disembarked us on the beach. We acclaimed him as our saviour and good angel. A little while later he brought in another ship, and then again another, and before evening had fallen we were in all five vessels saved by this godsend old man, the very reverse of Nauplius[5] in his actions, for the latter received the shipwrecked in a vastly different manner. On the following day other ships arrived, some of which had put out from

Alexandria the day before we set sail. So now we are quite a great fleet in a small harbour.

(trans. Fitzgerald – adapted)

*NOTES*

1 Sophocles, *Ajax* 1146.
2 *Odyssey*, IV. 511.
3 *Odyssey*, XI and XXIV.
4 *Iliad*, XXI. 281.
5 Nauplius, a son of Poseidon and king of Euboea, the father of Palamedes. As a revenge for the treatment his son had received at the hands of the Greeks he set up a burning torch on the promontory of Caphareus to deceive the Greek vessels that were sailing back from Troy, and thus caused their shipwreck on the coast.

### 219 Strabo VIII.6.20

Ancient navigation depended to a large extent on mountains and other landmarks on the coast. Ancient ships were therefore forced to remain close to the coast. This increased the dangers presented by cliffs and rocks. It was especially dangerous to round a stormy cape such as Cape Malea on the southern edge of the Peloponnese; this worked to the advantage of Corinth.

Corinth is called 'wealthy' because of its commerce, since it is situated on the Isthmus and is master of two harbours, of which the one leads straight to Asia, and the other to Italy; and it makes easy the exchange of merchandise from both countries that are so far distant from each other. And just as in early times the Strait of Sicily was not easy to navigate, so also the high seas, and particularly the sea beyond Malea, were not, on account of the contrary winds; and hence the proverb, 'But when you double Malea, forget your home.' At any rate, it was a welcome alternative, for the merchants both from Italy and from Asia, to avoid the voyage to Malea and to land their cargoes here.

(trans. Jones)

### 220 *SIG*[3] 1229

Sea-borne traffic between Asia Minor and Italy could not avoid this route, however. A merchant from Hierapolis in Phrygia had rounded this difficult cape several times. He was so proud of this achievement that he had it recorded on his tombstone.

Flavius Zeuxis, merchant, who sailed seventy-two times around Cape Malea to Italy, built this tomb for himself and his children, Flavius Theodorus and Flavius Theudas, and for any to whom they will give permission.

### 221 Strabo III.2.5

Augustus, the first emperor, paid a lot of attention to safety at sea. Although the Mediterranean was now cleared of enemy raids and pirates, Augustus established permanent war fleets in the navy bases of Ravenna and Misenum. Smaller flotillas were located in some minor harbours in the Mediterranean and on the Rhine and Danube. Within the Empire, piracy was reduced to a small-scale and incidental activity. Strabo put it briefly:

Added to that (sc. the regularity of the winds) is the peace nowadays, because all pirates are eliminated, and hence all sailors feel wholly at ease.

### 222 Suetonius, *Augustus* 98.2

Augustus' contribution to safety at sea was also recognized by professional sailors and their passengers.

As he had sailed through the Gulf of Puteoli, the passengers and crew of a recently arrived Alexandrian ship had put on white robes and garlands, burned incense, and wished him the greatest of good fortune – because, they said, they owed their lives to him and their liberty to sail the seas: in a word, their entire freedom and prosperity.

(trans. Graves)

# 22 Speed and duration of sea voyages

The speed of a sailing ship was largely dependent on the weather, and on the direction of the wind. Voyages from north to south could profit from the prevailing northerly winds in the summer months, and so be fairly speedy. Crossings in the opposite direction took much longer. It was not possible for ancient square-rigged ships to sail much closer to the wind than seven points, and they had to change tack fairly frequently. A journey from Alexandria to Rome could therefore take more than twice as long as the same trip in the other direction.

### 223 Pliny, *Natural History* XIX.3–4

In the nineteenth book of his *Naturalis Historia*, the elder Pliny praises the various qualities of flax. As one of its advantages he mentions that it was made into linen sails, which made possible sea-borne traffic. In this connection he lists several exceptionally fast sea journeys. We must realize, however, that these are record voyages made with favourable winds and that a speed of four and a half to six knots could not be reached by most merchantmen.

Is there a greater miracle than the flax plant which brings Egypt so close to Italy that of two governors of Egypt Galerius reached Alexandria on the seventh day from the straits of Messina, and Belbillus on the sixth, and that in the summer fifteen years later the praetorian senator Valerius Marianus crossed from Puteoli to Alexandria in nine days with a very gentle breeze? That there is a plant that brings Cadiz within seven days' sail from the straits of Gibraltar to Ostia, and thither Spain within four days and the Province of Narbonne within three, and Africa within two.

### 224 Achilles Tatius III.1.3–6

When the wind direction was unfavourable the speed of the ancient merchantmen with their square sails was probably not higher than 2 to

$2^1/2$ knots. The inconveniences to the crew during a trip against the wind were great.

> The ship heels over, laying one side in the water amidships and going high in the air on the other side; it is all aslant . . . . So we all change our position in the high side of the vessel . . . . Suddenly the wind leaps in the other side of the ship . . . . And a third time, a fourth time, many times, we go through the same procedure, keeping up with the gyrations of the ship.
>
> (trans. Casson)

# 23 Harbours

In the early days of shipping a natural bay or a sheltered beach sufficed as a mooring place; the smaller ships did not at any time need anything more sophisticated. The growth of transport by sea, and the increase in the size of ships, brought with them the need for improved harbour facilities.

### 225 Homer, *Odyssey* VI.262–9

Little is known about the earliest harbours of the Greeks. Homer's description of the harbour of the Phaeacians gives us some idea of how an eighth-century harbour may have looked; modern archaeological research has confirmed that provisions similar to those described by Homer existed. In this fragment, Nausicaä shows Odysseus around the town and the harbour.

But once we come to our city – it is surrounded by high battlements, it has an excellent harbour on each side and is approached by a narrow causeway, where the curved ships are drawn up to the road and each owner has his separate landing-place. Here is the people's meetingplace, built up next to the fine temple of Poseidon with blocks of quarried stone bedded deeply in the ground. It is here too that the sailors attend to the rigging of the black ships, their cables and sails, and smooth their oars. For the Phaeacians have no use for the bow and quiver, but only for masts and oars on the graceful craft they take pride in sailing across the grey seas.

(trans. Rieu)

### 226 Herodotus III.60

Trade in the Aegean increased during the seventh century, resulting in a growing need for improved harbour facilities. In the sixth century the tyrant Polycrates of Samos, whose power relied partly on his control of the sea (above, pp. 25ff.), ordered the construction of an immense breakwater that projected into the harbour more than 400 metres to a point where the sea is 35 metres deep. Herodotus' account is confirmed by the discovery of remnants of ancient breakwaters.

Secondly, there is the artificial harbour enclosed by a breakwater, which runs out into twenty fathoms of water and has a total length of over a quarter of a mile . . . .

(trans. De Sélincourt)

## 227 Plutarch, *Themistocles* XIX.2–4

In the fifth century, nearly all coastal towns could boast the possession of a well-equipped harbour with long quays where storehouses and offices were located. Various geographic situations were adapted for sheltering the ships. The busiest and most famous harbour was Piraeus, the port of Athens. There were two navy bases in Piraeus, where the Athenian war fleet of some 200–300 triremes docked. Merchants from all areas of the Mediterranean landed in the commercial harbour on the west side of Piraeus, which was a major commercial centre during the fifth and fourth centuries BC. The main objective of Themistocles in transferring, in 493 BC, the naval establishment from the open, indefensible beaches of Phaleron to the area enclosed by the promontory of Piraeus was a military one, but his achievements had enormous economic and political implications.

After this he (sc. Themistocles) equipped the Piraeus; he had noticed the excellent shape of its harbours, and he wished to marry the whole city to the sea. In this his policy was somewhat at variance with that of the ancient Athenian kings: they, as is said, in their efforts to tear the citizens away from the sea and accustom them to live not by sailing but by agriculture, spread the story about Athena, how when Poseidon was contending with her for possession of the country she defeated him by showing the judges her sacred olive-tree. But Themistocles did not, as Aristophanes the comic poet states, 'knead the Piraeus on to the city',[1] on the contrary, it was the city that he fastened on the Piraeus, and the land to the sea. And so he strengthened the common people at the expense of the aristocracy, and filled men with boldness, since power was now coming into the hands of sailors and boatswains and helmsmen. Therefore it was, too, that the speakers' rostrum on the Pnyx, which had been made so as to look towards the sea, was later turned round by the Thirty and made to look inland: their belief was that a maritime empire brought about democracy, whereas oligarchy was less distasteful to men who farmed the land.

*NOTE*

1 Aristophanes, *Knights* 815.

## 228 Pausanias I.1.2–3

In the second century AD the travel writer Pausanias visited Piraeus, and recorded what was left of the glorious past.

Piraeus was a community from ancient times, but not a port until Themistocles was governor of Athens. Phaleron, where the sea and city are nearest, was the port, and it was from Phaleron that they say Menestheus and his ships put out for Troy, and Theseus before him set sail to pay Minos the penalty for the death of Androgeos. When Themistocles came to power he made Piraeus the port as he thought it was better sited for shipping, and because it had three harbours as opposed to the one at Phaleron. Down to my time the boat-sheds were still standing there, and beside the biggest harbour was the tomb of Themistocles. The story goes that the Athenians regretted the way they had treated him, and his family brought home his bones from Magnesia; certainly his children did return to Athens: they dedicated a painting in the Parthenon which has Themistocles in it.

(trans. Levi)

## 229 Demosthenes, *Against Lacritus* 28

It was not very difficult to avoid paying the harbour duties, or evade other trade laws. Smugglers could use a little bay east of Piraeus, known as the 'Thieves' Harbour'.

You must now hear the most outrageous thing which this fellow Lacritus has done; for it was he who managed the whole affair. When they arrived here they did not put into your port, but came to anchor in Thieves' Harbour, which is outside of the signs marking your port; and to anchor in Thieves' Harbour is the same as if one were to anchor in Aegina or Megara; for anyone can sail forth from that harbour to whatever point he wishes and at any moment he pleases. Well, their vessel lay at anchor there for more than twenty-five days, and these men walked about in your sample-market.

## 230 *IG* XII suppl. 348

In the third century BC traffic in the port of Thasos had become so heavy that the authorities instituted a law allocating different moorings to different types of ship. The harbour was divided into two basins reserved exclusively for ships of more than 5,000 talents (ca. 130 tons) and 3,000 talents respectively. For smaller boats, of less than 60 tons, which were used by farmers for the transport of goods to the market, moorings were reserved elsewhere.

No ship with a tonnage of less than 3,000 talents (ca. seventy-eight tons) may be hauled up within the boundaries of the first, and no ship under 5,000 talents (ca. 130 tons) may be hauled up beyond the second; anyone who breaks these rules and hauls up his ship, shall pay a fine of five staters to the city.

### 231 Appian, *Punic Wars* 96

In the fourth century, harbours such as Carthage and Syracuse grew in importance. The Sicilian tyrants took great care to improve the naval base as well as the commercial port. The result of their efforts was a very impressive harbour, with separate basins. The artificial harbour of Carthage played an important role in the life of the town. Appian gives a reliable description of this harbour.

The harbours had communication with each other, and a common entrance from the sea seventy feet wide, which could be closed with iron chains. The first port was for merchant vessels, and here were collected all kinds of ships' tackle. Within the second port was an island, and great quays were set at intervals round both the harbour and the island. These embankments were full of shipyards which had capacity for 220 vessels. In addition to them were magazines for their tackle and furniture. Two Ionic columns stood in front of each dock, giving the appearance of a continuous portico to both the harbour and the island. On the island was built the admiral's house, from which the trumpeter gave signals, the herald delivered orders, and the admiral himself overlooked everything. The island lay near the entrance to the harbour, and rose to a considerable height, so that the admiral could observe what was going on at sea, while those who were approaching by water could not get any clear view of what took place within. Not even incoming merchants could see the docks at once, for a double wall enclosed them, and there were gates by which merchant ships could pass from the first port to the city without traversing the dockyards. Such was the appearance of Carthage at that time.

(trans. White)

### 232 Strabo XVII.1.6–9

In the Hellenistic period several new harbours were constructed to suit the ambitions of the Hellenistic rulers and to meet the demands of growing trade. In 330 BC Alexander the Great gave his name to a new port that was to be constructed on the Mediterranean coast of Egypt after a design by the Greek Democrates. Alexandria was the most successful and most famous of the new harbours. The geographer Strabo gives a full description.

The sea-coast, then, from Pelusium, as one sails towards the west, as far as the Canobic mouth, is about one thousand three hundred stadia – the 'base' of the Delta, as I have called it; and thence to the island Pharos, one hundred and fifty stadia more. Pharos is an oblong isle, is very close to the mainland, and forms with it a harbour with two mouths; for the shore of the mainland forms a bay, since it thrusts two promontories into the open sea, and between these is situated the island, which closes the bay, for it lies lengthwise parallel to the shore. Of the extremities of Pharos, the eastern one lies closer to the mainland and to the promontory opposite it (the promontory called Lochias), and thus makes the harbour narrow at the mouth; and in addition to the narrowness of the intervening passage there are also rocks, some under the water, and others projecting out of it, which at all hours roughen the waves that strike them from the open sea. And likewise the extremity of the isle is a rock, which is washed all round by the sea and has upon it a tower that is admirably constructed of white marble with many stories and bears the same name as the island. This was an offering made by Sostratus of Cnidos, a friend of the kings, for the safety of mariners, as the inscription says: for since the coast was harbourless and low on either side, and also had reefs and shallows, those who were sailing from the open sea thither needed some lofty and conspicuous sign to enable them to direct their course aright to the entrance of the harbour. And the western mouth is also not easy to enter, although it does not require so much caution as the other. And it likewise forms a second harbour, that of Eunostus, as it is called, which lies in front of the closed harbour which was dug by the hand of man. For the harbour which affords the entrance on the side of the above-mentioned tower of Pharos is the Great Harbour, whereas these two lie continuous with that harbour in their innermost recess, being separated from it only by the embankment called the *Heptastadium*. The embankment forms a bridge extending from the mainland to the western portion of the island, and leaves open only two passages into the harbour of Eunostus, which are bridged over. However, this work formed not only a bridge to the island but also an aqueduct, at least when Pharos was inhabited. But in these present times it has been laid waste by the deified Caesar in his war against the Alexandrians, since it had sided with the kings. A few seamen, however, live near the tower. As for the Great Harbour, in addition to its being beautifully enclosed both by the embankment and by nature, it is not only so deep close to the shore that the largest ship can be moored at the steps, but also is cut up into several harbours. Now the earlier kings of the Aegyptians, being content with what they had and not wanting foreign imports at all, and being prejudiced against all who sailed the seas, and particularly against the Greeks (for owing to scarcity of land of their own the Greeks were ravagers and coveters of that of others), set a guard over this region and ordered it to keep away any who should approach; and they gave them as a place of abode Rhacotis, as it is called, which is now that part of the city of the Alexandrians which lies above the ship-houses, but was at that time a village; and they gave over the parts round about the village to herdsmen, who likewise were able to prevent the approach of outsiders. But when Alexander visited the place and saw the advantages of the site, he resolved to fortify the city on the harbour. Writers record, as a sign of the good fortune that has since attended the city, an incident which occurred at the time of tracing the lines of the foundation: When the architects were marking the lines of the enclosure with chalk, the supply of chalk gave out; and when the king arrived, his stewards furnished a part of the barley-meal which had been prepared for the workmen, and by means of this the streets also, to a larger number than before, were laid out. This occurrence, then, they are said to have interpreted as a good omen.

The advantages of the city's site are various; for, first, the place is washed by two seas, on the north by the Aegyptian Sea, as it is called, and on the south by Lake Mareia, also called Mareotis. This is filled by many canals from the Nile, both from above and on the sides, and through these canals the imports are much larger than those from the sea, so that the harbour on the lake was in fact richer than that on the sea, and here the exports from Alexandria also are larger than the imports; and anyone might judge, if he were at either Alexandria or Dicaearchia and saw the merchant vessels both at their arrival and at their departure, how much heavier or lighter they sailed thither or therefrom.

(trans. Jones)

### 233 Flavius Josephus, *Jewish War* I 408–13

At the end of the first century BC Herodes, king of Judea, built a new city, Caesarea, on the Palestinian coast, and created a harbour which, according to Flavius Josephus, surpassed Piraeus.

His notice was attracted by a town on the coast, called Strato's Tower, which, though then in a state of decay, was, from its admirable situation, suited for the exercise of his liberality. He rebuilt it entirely with limestone, and adorned it with the most magnificent palaces, displaying here, as nowhere else, the liveliness of his imagination.

For the whole shore from Dora to Joppa, midway between which the city lies, was without a harbour, so that vessels bound for Egypt along the coast of Phoenicia had to ride at anchor in the open when threatened by the south-west wind; for even a moderate breeze from this quarter dashes the waves to such a height against the rocks, that the backwash spreads a wild commotion far out to sea. However, by lavish expenditure and enterprise, the king triumphed over nature and constructed a harbour larger than the Piraeus, with further deep roadsteps in its recesses.

Notwithstanding the totally recalcitrant nature of the site, he wrestled with the difficulties so successfully, that the solidity of his masonry defied the sea, while its beauty was such as if no obstacle had existed. Having marked out the area for a harbour of the size mentioned, he lowered blocks of stone into twenty fathoms of water, most of them measuring fifty feet in length by nine in depth and ten in breadth, some being even bigger. Upon the submarine foundation thus laid he constructed above the surface a mole 200 feet broad; of which 100 were built out to break the force of the waves, whence this portion was called the breakwater, while the remainder supported a stone wall encircling the harbour. From this wall arose, at intervals, massive towers, the most conspicuous and most magnificent of which was called Drusium after the stepson of Caesar.

A row of arched recesses provided landing-places for mariners putting in to harbour, while the whole circular terrace in front of these served as a broad promenade for disembarking passengers. The entrance to the port faced northwards, because in these latitudes the north wind is the most favourable of all. At the harbour-mouth stood colossal statues, three on either side, resting on pillars; those on the left of ships entering port were supported by a massive tower, those on the right by two upright blocks of stone clamped together, whose height exceeded that of the tower on the other side. Adjoining the harbour were houses, also of limestone, and upon it converged the streets of the town, laid at equal distances apart.

### 234 Vitruvius, *On Architecture* V.12.2–3

Vitruvius, a Roman architect, gives some information about the construction of harbours in his guide to Hellenistic and Roman practice in town-planning, architecture and civil engineering.

The masonry which is to be in the sea is to be constructed in this way. Earth is to be brought from the district which runs from Cumae to the promontory of Minerva, and mixed in the mortar, two parts to one of lime. Then in the place marked out, cofferdams, formed of oak piles and tied together with chains, are to be let down into the water and firmly fixed. Next the lower part between them under the water is to be levelled and cleared with a platform of small beams laid across and the work is to be carried up with stones and mortar as above described, until the space for the structure between the dams is filled.

(trans. Granger)

### 235 Cassius Dio LX.11.1–5

The largest harbour of antiquity was Portus, the harbour of Ostia, some 30 kilometres from Rome. The mouth of the Tiber was not a natural harbour; there was only a sandy beach at which large ships could not moor. During the Republic, Puteoli, in Campania, served as a transit harbour, where cargoes were transferred to smaller vessels that could land in Ostia. Cargoes were also sometimes transferred in the open sea and brought ashore in small launches. Caesar and Augustus had already made plans to provide Rome with the harbour it deserved, but construction had to wait till AD 42, when the emperor Claudius gave the final go-ahead. Ostia became a prosperous town of some 60,000 inhabitants.

On the occasion of a severe famine he considered the problem of providing an abundant food-supply, not only for that particular crisis but for all future time. For practically all the grain used by the Romans was imported, and yet the region near the mouth of the Tiber had no safe landing-places or suitable harbours, so that their mastery of the sea was rendered useless to them. Except for the cargoes brought in during the summer season and stored in warehouses, they had no supplies for the winter; for if any one ever risked a voyage at that season, he was sure to meet with disaster. In view of this situation, Claudius undertook to construct a harbour, and would not be deterred even when the architects, upon his enquiring how great the cost would be, answered, 'You don't want to do it!' so confident were they that the huge expenditures necessary would shake him from his purpose, if he should learn the cost beforehand. He, however, conceived an undertaking worthy of the dignity and greatness of Rome, and he brought it to accomplishment. In the first place, he excavated a very considerable tract of land, built retaining walls on every side of the excavation, and then let the sea into it; secondly, in the sea itself he constructed huge moles on both sides of the entrance and thus enclosed a large body of water, in the midst of which he reared an island and placed on it a tower with a beacon light. This harbour, then, as it is still called in local parlance, was created by him at this time.

(trans. Cary)

## 236 Pliny, *Letters* VI.31.15–17

Claudius' harbour had a surface of more than 80 hectares, and was protected by two moles with a length of about 700 metres. It was now possible for the large grain ships to anchor in Ostia. The harbour was constantly threatened by silt, however, and the largest ships continued to have problems with access to the port. Another problem was that Claudius' harbour did not offer sufficient protection against bad weather, as became clear in AD 62 when about 200 grain-ships sank in the harbour. In the early second century AD the emperor Trajan decided to build a new harbour, with a surface of about 33 hectares, between the old harbour of Claudius and the mouth of the Tiber. The younger Pliny, who was staying in a house in Centum Cellae (modern Civita Vecchia), provides an eye-witness account of the construction works.

Here is a villa, surrounded by the most verdant meadows, and overhanging a bay of the coast where they are at this moment constructing a harbour. The left-hand mole of this port is protected by immensely solid masonry; the right is now being completed. An island is rising in the mouth of the harbour, which will break the force of the waves when the wind blows shorewards, and afford passage to ships on either side. Its construction is highly worth seeing; huge stones are transported hither in a broad-bottomed vessel, and being sunk one upon the other, are fixed by their own weight, gradually accumulating in the manner, as it were, of a rampart. It already lifts its rocky back above the ocean, while the waves which beat upon it, being tossed to an immense height, roar prodigiously, and whiten all the sea round. To these stones are added wooden piles, which in time will give it the appearance of a natural island. This port will be, and already is, named after its great author, and will prove of infinite benefit, by affording a haven to ships on a long stretch of harbourless coast. Farewell.

(trans. Melmoth)

## 237 Properce I.14.1–4

In all larger harbours there were numerous small boats and launches to bring cargo and passengers ashore. In Ostia there were also special vessels to carry goods from the port to the city of Rome along the winding Tiber, a distance of about 30 kilometres. The large *codiciariae* were usually towed upstream, but the smaller types, such as the *linter*, could be sailed or rowed. The poet Properce describes the busy traffic on the Tiber.

Though reclining idly by Tiber's wave you drink Lesbian wine from cups chased by the hand of Mentor, and marvel now how swiftly the small boats (*lintres*) run by and now how slowly the barges (*codiciariae*) go along on their towlines.

### 238 *SEG* XIX 684

Damage to the harbour facilities and silting could also be the result of human activities. In response to the damage done by the importers of building materials, the governor of the Roman province of Asia issued a decree in AD 161.

To Good Fortune. The Proconsul, Lucius Antonius Albus proclaims. Since it is necessary for the greatest metropole of Asia, and well nigh for the entire world, that the harbour, which receives people landing there from all over the world, should not be obstructed; when I learned in what manner people cause damage to the harbour, I thought it necessary to prohibit this by means of an edict and set a fitting penalty for those who disobey. I order therefore, that the importers of wood and of marble neither store the wood along the quays, nor saw the marble. For the first cause damage to the pillars which were constructed for the protection of the harbour by the weight of their cargoes, and the latter, by throwing in the emery . . . fill up the riverbed and block the stream; both categories obstruct the traffic on the quay.

Since Marcellus, the secretary (sc. of the city) acting under my orders, was not able to put a stop to their insolence, let it be known to them that if anyone who is not aware of this edict is caught doing one of the things that have been prohibited, he is to pay (. . . amount not stated) to the most distinguished city of the Ephesians, and no less is he to give account to me personally. For, since our great Emperor has shown concern for the protection of the harbour, and since he has continuously been sending dispatches on this matter, it is not right that people who ruin the harbour should be let off merely by paying a fine.

Let this edict be announced.

The secretary was Tiberius Claudius Polydeuces Marcellus, Asiarch.

# Select bibliography

We have included in this bibliography only the books and articles which have special importance for the main themes of this book.

Austin, M.M. and Vidal-Naquet, P. *Economic and Social History of Ancient Greece, An Introduction*, London 1972.

Basch, L. *Le Musée imaginaire de la marine antique*, Athens 1987.

Bass, G. (ed.) *A History of Seafaring Based on Underwater Archaeology*, London 1972.

Casson, L. *Ships and Seamanship in the Ancient World*, Princeton 1972.

Casson, L. *Travel in the Ancient World*, London 1974.

Casson, L. *The Periplus Maris Erythraei*, Princeton 1989.

Charlesworth, M.P. *Trade-routes and Commerce of the Ancient World*, Cambridge 1924.

Chevallier, R. *Roman Roads*, London 1976.

D'Arms, J.H. *Commerce and Social Standing in Ancient Rome*, Cambridge (Mass.) 1981.

D'Arms, J.H. and Kopff, E.C. (eds) *The Seaborne Commerce of Ancient Rome*, Rome 1984.

Drexhage, H.J. *Preise, Mieten/Pachten, Kosten und Löhne im Römischen Aegypten bis zum Regierungsantritt Diokletians*, Münster 1991.

Duncan-Jones, R.P. *The Economy of the Roman Empire. Quantitative Studies*, Cambridge 1974.

Duncan-Jones, R.P. *Structure and Scale in the Roman Economy*, Cambridge 1990.

Finley, M.I. *The Ancient Economy*, Berkeley 1985.

Frank, T. *An Economic Survey of Ancient Rome*, 5 vols, Baltimore 1933–40.

Frayn, J.M. *Sheep Rearing and the Wool Trade in Italy during the Roman Period*, Liverpool 1984.

Friedländer, L. *Darstellungen aus der Sittengeschichte Roms*, 4 vols, Leipzig 1919–22.

Garnsey, P.D.A. (ed.) *Non-slave Labour in the Graeco-Roman World*, Cambridge 1980.

Garnsey, P.D.A. *Famine and Food Supply in the Graeco-Roman World*, Cambridge 1988.

Garnsey, P.D.A., Hopkins, K. and Whittaker, C.R. (eds) *Trade in the Ancient Economy*, Cambridge 1983.

Garnsey, P.D.A. and Saller, R. *The Roman Empire: Economy, Society and Culture*, London 1987.

Garnsey, P.D.A. and Whittaker, C.R. (eds) *Trade and Famine in Classical Antiquity*, Cambridge 1983.

Gianfrotta, P.A. and Pomey, P. *Archeologia Subacquea*, Milan 1981.

Göttlicher, A. *Die Schiffe der Antike. Eine Einführung in die Archäologie der Wasserfahrzeuge*, Berlin 1985.

Greene, K. *The Archaeology of the Roman Economy*, London 1986.

Hasebroek, J. *Staat und Handel im alten Griechenland*, Tübingen 1928.

Höckmann, O. *Antike Seefahrt*, Munich 1985.

Hopkins, K. 'Economic growth and towns in classical antiquity', in Ph. Abrams and E.A. Wrigley (eds) *Towns in Societies*, Cambridge 1978, 35–77.

Hopkins, K. 'Taxes and trade in the Roman empire', *JRS* 70 (1980), 101–25.

McGrail, S. *Sources and Techniques in Boat Archaeology*, Oxford 1977.

Manacorda, D. 'The ager Cosanus and the production of the amphorae of Sestius', *JRS* 68 (1978), 122–31.

Meiggs, R. *The Athenian Empire*, Oxford 1972.

Meiggs, R. *Roman Ostia*, Oxford 1973.

Meiggs, R. *Trees and Timber in the Ancient Mediterranean World*, Oxford 1982.

Meijer, F. *A History of Seafaring in the Classical World*, London 1986.

Muckelroy, K. (ed.) *Archaeology under Water. An Atlas of the World's Submerged Sites*, New York–London 1980.

Ormerod, H.A. *Piracy in the Ancient World*, Liverpool 1976.

Pleket, H.W. 'Urban elites and the economy in the Greek cities of the Roman empire', *Münstersche Beiträge zur antiken Handelsgeschichte* 3 (1984), 3–37.

Pleket, H.W. 'Wirtschaft', in W. Fisher, J.A. van Houtte, H. Kellenbenz, I. Mieck and F. Vittinghoff (eds) *Handbuch der Europäischen Wirtschafts- und Sozialgeschichte*, Band 1, *Wirtschaft und Gesellschaft des Imperium Romanum*, Stuttgart 1990, 25–160.

Pomey, P. and Tchernia, A. 'Le tonnage maximum des navires de commerce Romains', *Archaeonautica* 2 (1978), 233–51.

Purcell, N. 'Wine and wealth in ancient Italy', *JRS* 75 (1985), 10–23.

Rickman, G. *The Corn Supply of Ancient Rome*, Oxford 1980.

Rougé, J. *L'Organisation du commerce maritime en méditerranée sous l'empire romain*, Paris 1966.

Roztovtzeff, M. *The Social and Economic History of the Hellenistic World*, Oxford 1941.

Roztovtzeff, M. *The Social and Economic History of the Roman Empire*, Oxford 1957.

Throckmorton, P. (ed.) *History from the Sea. Shipwrecks and Archaeology*, London 1987.

Ward-Perkins, J.B. 'Quarrying in antiquity. Technology, tradition and social change', *Proceedings of the British Academy* 57 (1971), 137–58.

Warmington, E.H. *The Commerce between the Roman Empire and India*, London 1974.

White, K.D. *Greek and Roman Technology*, London 1984.

Will, E.L. 'The Sestius amphoras: a reappraisal', *Journal of Field Archaeology* 6 (1979), 339–50.

# Index of passages cited

**Inscriptions**

**Papyri**



**Legal sources**

# General index

46297923R00125

Made in the USA
Lexington, KY
24 July 2019